YE SHALL RECEIVE POWER FROM ON HIGH

A BIBLE STUDY ON THE BAPTISM IN THE HOLY GHOST

by Gwen R. Shaw

Engeltal Press
P.O. Box 447
Jasper, AR 72641
U.S.A.

Copyright by Gwen R. Shaw 1987
End-Time Handmaidens
P.O. Box 447
Jasper, AR 72641

Printed in the United States of America

FOREWORD

For long centuries the prophets foresaw a glorious hour when the Holy Spirit would visit the sons of men—not only to be with them, but to be in them. This special visitation was called the "promise of the Father." Before returning to Heaven, Jesus' final directive to His disciples specifically warned they were to **go nowhere, nor do anything** until **after** they had received this promise. It is apparent that the deliberate thrust of Calvary has been, and yet remains, to prepare a people for this one consuming purpose: that God, the Holy Spirit, might indwell human temple-vessels. In Galatians 3:13, 14 Paul tells us that Christ has redeemed us from the curse of the Law, having become a curse for us...**in order that** in Christ the blessing of Abraham might come—**so that** we might receive the promise of the Spirit through faith.

Jesus died that we might be reborn, **but reborn to the end** that we receive His mighty indwelling. Yet sadly, to this hour much of the church labors ignorant of Christ's mandate that we be filled with the Spirit; and though we have new wine skins furnished through regeneration, we are barren and fruitless, never having received Him who is the new wine.

It is therefore with deep gratitude that we welcome this new book from Sister Gwen on the subject of the Holy Spirit, that very One who has unctioned her so mightily during four decades of ministry throughout the earth.

Having been privileged to labor with Sister Gwen in some of these fields, I can readily testify to the apostolic anointing God has long entrusted to this, His daughter. I therefore know of no one more qualified to write on the subject of the Holy Spirit than she. How fortunate for us all that she has at last set down this practical Bible study in which she shares vital truths and Scriptural keys to her blessed life and service under the personal Lordship of that ever-present omnipotent One, who has been her constant Comforter and mighty Helper, God, the Holy Spirit!

June Lewis

INTRODUCTION

Has your heart felt dry and barren? Do you feel that God is far away? Have you longed for God to use you in a wonderful new way? Does the enemy accuse you of being dead and cold? Are you tired of your spiritual condition and long for a new touch of God on your life?

Then, my friend, there is hope for you, for God cannot do anything with anyone who is self-complacent and contented with his status-quo. It takes our desperation, born out of sincerity, together with an honest cry to God, for Him to answer us and pour out His Spirit upon us from on high, so that we can receive power, even the power from on high which He has promised us.

This Bible study is intended only for the sincere seeker who is honest enough with himself to confess, "I need more of God in my life. I know I don't have all that God has for me." If you can be that honest with yourself, then read on, for your heart is open to receive.

Jesus said, *"Blessed are they which do **hunger** and thirst after righteousness, for they shall be filled."* (Matthew 5:6)

The Holy Spirit is the source of all life and power (Genesis 1:2). It is only by the infilling of the Holy Spirit in your life that your soul can be satisfied. So come to the waters and drink, and you shall never thirst again (John 4:14).

Gwen R. Shaw

TABLE OF CONTENTS

Chapter		Page
One	The Dispensations of the Holy Trinity	1
Two	The Promise Is To You	6
Three	The Holy Spirit is the Key to Power	15
Four	The Bible Account of the Baptism of the Holy Spirit	21
Five	Why Has Satan Fought the Truth of the Experience of Speaking in Tongues?	28
Six	How Does Satan Fight Speaking in Tongues?	36
Seven	Scriptures Which Refer to the Baptism of the Holy Spirit	40
Eight	Hindrances to Receiving the Baptism of the Holy Spirit	46
Nine	Paul's Instruction Regarding the Holy Spirit to the Church at Corinth	51
Ten	The Nine Fruits of the Holy Spirit	56
Eleven	The Nine Gifts of the Spirit	62
Twelve	Questions and Answers	73
Conclusion		81

CHAPTER ONE

THE DISPENSATIONS OF THE HOLY TRINITY

The Baptism of the Holy Spirit has become the most controversial of all the church doctrines. And yet, it should be so simple that even a child could understand and receive this wonderful, God-promised experience.

I believe Satan himself has fought this truth because he knows that without the power of the Holy Spirit we are a church that will exist in disunity, disarray and be powerless against evil. Without the Holy Spirit we are nothing.

The Dispensation of the Father

The Old Testament was the dispensation of God the Father. He revealed Himself as the Father of Abraham, Isaac, Jacob, the Children of Israel and us all. In four thousand years men learned to know the Father. He talked with Moses on Mount Sinai, shook the mountains, divided the seas and destroyed His enemies.

The Dispensation of the Son

Then He sent His Son Jesus and the dispensation of the Son began. For 33 1/2 years He lived and walked among us, showing us the love of God in a new way, teaching us, healing our sicknesses, raising our dead and then dying for us. Both before He died and again after His resurrection He promised that He would send the Third Person of the Trinity, the Holy Ghost.

In the Old Testament God came down and talked to man from time to time. That was the *Dispensation of the Father*.

In the *Dispensation of Jesus Christ* He communed with man and taught man the truths of Heaven.

The Dispensation of the Holy Spirit

But in the *Dispensation of the Holy Spirit* He came to dwell **in** man, not **with** him, but **in** him. That is what Jesus meant when He said, *"And I will pray the Father, and he shall give you another Comforter, that he may abide with you for ever; Even the Spirit of truth; whom the world cannot receive, because it seeth him not, neither knoweth him: but ye know him; for he dwelleth with you, and shall be in you."* (John 14:16, 17)

In this dispensation the office work of the Third Person of the Holy Trinity is to dwell **within** us. He literally comes inside of us and uses our bodies to do the works of God, just like He used the body of Jesus to do the works of God.

Jesus Did His Mighty Works Through the Power of the Holy Ghost

In Acts 10:38 we read Peter's sermon to Cornelius which he preached in Caesaria. There Peter clearly reveals the source of Jesus' great power to live a pure life and to do the mighty works of God, *"How God anointed Jesus of Nazareth with the Holy Ghost and with power: who went about doing good, and healing all that were oppressed of the devil; for God was with him."*

It was through the anointing of the Holy Ghost (which the Father had given Him) that Jesus was enabled to do the mighty works of God.

We know that Jesus was mightily filled with the Holy Spirit, because Jesus Himself bore witness to this fact when He spoke to Nicodemus, *"For he whom God hath sent speaketh the words of God: for God giveth not the Spirit by measure unto him. The Father loveth the Son, and hath given all things into his hand."* (John 3:34, 35)

Yes, Jesus had the entire fullness of the Holy Spirit in His earthly life. In Luke 4:1 we read that after Jesus was baptized by John the Baptist, and the Holy Spirit in the form of a dove came and sat upon Him, *"...Jesus being full of the Holy Ghost returned from Jordan, and was led by the Spirit into the wilderness."* And then again, after His victory over Satan, *"...Jesus returned in the power of the Spirit into Galilee: and there went out a fame of him through all the region round about. And he taught in their synagogues, being glorified of all."* (Luke 4:14, 15) It was this great power of the Holy Ghost in His life that made Him famous, for He not only did the mighty miracles of God, He spoke the oracle of God in a way that man had never ever heard. All this was by the power of the Holy Ghost by Whom He was indwelt. Paul, trying to describe this truth, says in Colossians 1:19 and 2:9, *"For in him dwelleth all the fulness of the Godhead bodily."*

Remember, we read in John 3:34, 35 that John said that Jesus had received the Holy Spirit from the Father because the Father loved Him.

The Father Loves You, Too

You say, "What chance do I have? How can the Father love me in this same way as He loved His Son?"

Listen to what Jesus tells us about the Father's love for us:

"...he that loveth me shall be loved of my Father ..." (John 14:21)

"...If a man love me, he will keep my words: and my Father will love him, and we will come unto him, and make our abode with him." (John 14:23)

"For the Father himself loveth you, because ye have loved me, and have believed that I came out from God." (John 16:27)

"...and hast loved them, as thou hast loved me." (John 17:23)

You see, the Father has a very special love in His heart for us. It is even the same love that He had for His Son. So shall He not also freely give us all things, even as He gave His Holy Spirit unto His Son (Romans 8:32)?

Do not allow unbelief or erroneous teaching to rob you of the promises of God. Break through to receive all that God meant for you to have, because this is the dispensation of the Holy Ghost. You need to give place in your life to the Holy Ghost and let Him work the works of God in and through you. Only then can God do His wonderful works in these last days so that the dispensation of the Son, which was cut off (Daniel 9:26) in the midst of His years, can be completed in the Millenium when He shall reign as King of kings and Lord of lords (Revelation 11:15, 17:14).

STUDY QUESTIONS

1. Why has the subject of the Baptism of the Holy Spirit become controversial?

2. Explain the differences between the three dispensations of the Godhead.

3. How did Jesus do His mighty works?

4. What rights do we have to ask God for the same baptism of power?

5. When will the Son of God continue His dispensation?

6. Memorize Acts 10:38.

7. Read Acts 1 and 2.

CHAPTER TWO

THE PROMISE IS TO YOU

We have received our initial promise of the Holy Spirit through the words of Jesus Christ Himself. The last night in the Upper Room He promised His disciples that He was going to ask the Father to send the Holy Spirit. Let us look again at some of the things He said concerning this promise.

The Holy Spirit Reveals Truth to Us

The first words were those we have already quoted from John 14:16, 17. Let us read them again, *"And I will pray the Father, and he shall give you another Comforter, that he may abide with you for ever; Even the Spirit of truth; whom the world cannot receive, because it seeth him not, neither knoweth him: but ye know him; for he dwelleth with you, and shall be in you."*

Here the Holy Spirit is called the **Spirit of Truth**. That means that He will teach and reveal truth to us because He will live in us.

The Holy Spirit Is Our Comforter and Teacher

"But the Comforter, which is the Holy Ghost, whom the Father will send in my name, he shall teach you all things, and bring all things to your remembrance, whatsoever I have said unto you." (John 14:26)

Here the Holy Spirit is called the **Comforter**. He is always present to give us comfort and encouragement. Not only that, He also is our **Teacher,** even as Jesus was the "Rabbi" who taught His disciples. And then, to top it all off, the Holy Spirit who lives in us, reminds us of the truths which we have learned, thus enabling us also to be teachers ("rabbis") of the Word.

Do you have a poor memory? Ask the Holy Spirit to help you. Truths that have entered your spirit are "programmed" into your spirit for eternity. What you have learned with your carnal mind you may forget, but your spirit will never forget what it has learned, for the Holy Spirit lives in your spirit to remind it what you have been taught. These truths will even stay with you if you are in a coma or after death.

The Holy Spirit Reveals that Jesus Is the Son of God

John 15:26, *"But when the Comforter is come, whom I will send unto you from the Father, even the Spirit of truth, which proceedeth from the Father, he shall testify of me:"*

For you and me it is easy to believe that Jesus is the Messiah. But for the Jews or the Moslems it is very difficult because they have been taught against this truth from childhood. It is therefore impossible for them to be convinced through testimony or argument. The only One who can reveal Jesus to them is the Holy Spirit. Therefore we need to pray mightily for the Holy Spirit to reveal Jesus Christ to the seed of Abraham, both Isaac's and Ishmael's.

The Holy Spirit Convicts of Sin and Warns of its Consequences

John 16:7, 8, *"Nevertheless I tell you the truth; It is expedient for you that I go away: for if I go not away, the Comforter will not come unto you; but if I depart, I will send him unto you. And when he is come, he will reprove the world of sin, and of righteousness, and of judgment."*

Of Sin: This generation is destroying itself because it has no guilt in spite of all its sin. Why is there such a lack of guilt?

How can so-called Christians sin so grievously and feel no condemnation? Is it because the Holy Spirit has left them? Has He ceased convicting men of their sins?

Surely it is the goodness of God which leads us to repentance (Romans 2:4). Therefore, if God loves us, He will send His Holy Spirit to convict us when we sin. If, in spite of sin, we feel no guilt or conviction, we are on dangerous ground.

Of Righteousness: He is the One who gives us the pure desire to live a holy and righteous life. If this desire is gone, then the Holy Spirit has left us.

Of Judgment: The reckless attitude of this mocking generation, which is rushing headlong to the judgment and hell, is true evidence that the Holy Spirit has left sinners to their own devices. Paul, speaking of this wicked generation in the first chapter of Romans says, *"Wherefore God also gave them up to uncleanness, through the lusts of their own hearts, to dishonour their own bodies themselves."* (Romans 1:24)

"For this cause God gave them up unto vile affections (passions)*: for even their women did change the natural use into that which is against nature."* (Romans 1:26)

Therefore, my friend, if the Holy Spirit convicts you of sin, be grateful to God and ask Him to forgive you and give you the strength to resist temptation.

The Holy Spirit Is Our Guide

John 16:13, 14, *"Howbeit when he, the Spirit of truth, is come, he will **guide you** into all truth: for he shall not speak of himself; but whatsoever he shall hear, that shall he speak: and he will show you things to come. He shall glorify me: for he shall receive of mine, and shall show it unto you."*

The Work of the Holy Spirit Resembles the Work of Jesus

How closely the work of the Holy Spirit resembles the work of Jesus! In John 8:26 He said, *"I have many things to say and to judge of you: but he that sent me is true; and I speak to the world those things which I have heard of him."* No wonder the spies who followed him said, *"...Never man spake like this man."* (John 7:46)

Jesus received His instructions from the Father. The Holy Spirit also receives His instructions from the Father. His work is to reveal to us things to come, through the inspired word of prophecy, and also to glorify Jesus by making Jesus real to us and precious to our hearts. Oh, thank God for the wonderful work of the Holy Spirit!

John 20:21, 22, *"Then said Jesus to them again, Peace be unto you: as my Father hath sent me, even so send I you. And when he had said this, he breathed on them, and saith unto them, Receive ye the Holy Ghost."*

After He rose from the dead, Jesus visited His disciples not only to show Himself alive but also to remind them of things He had taught them in the Upper Room (only a few days earlier) that the time had come for them to receive the Holy Spirit in their lives.

The Command Is Also to You

Luke 24:49, *"And, behold, I send the promise of my Father upon you: but tarry ye in the city of Jerusalem, until ye be endued with power from on high."*

Jesus not only gave us the **promise** of the enduement of power which comes through the Holy Spirit. He also commanded us to be filled. We must not ignore nor disregard

His command! If we are true followers of Jesus Christ, we are obliged to obey His commands to us. He said, *"Ye are my friends, if ye do whatsoever I command you."* (John 15:14)

Jesus told them that the time had come for them to take the message of the Gospel to all the world. After opening their understanding so that they could understand the Scriptures (Luke 24:45), He said the time had come that the message of repentance and remission of sins should be preached in His Name among all nations, beginning at Jerusalem (Luke 24:47). Because they had been witnesses of His life, death and resurrection, they had a responsibility to take this Gospel message of salvation to the world. There was no more time left for intensive years of theological training, saving up money to go or any other delays. The time to go had come. But before they went they had to be endued with power for their missions. And so they were **commanded** to tarry in Jerusalem until they would receive this "promise of the Father."

He knew that without the Holy Spirit they could do nothing. It was not an experience they should "take by faith" like salvation, and step out, trusting that this definite work of grace had been done in their lives.

Sad to say, many do just that. They accept salvation by faith, which is good and proper, for Ephesians 2:8 says, *"For by grace are ye saved through faith; and that not of yourselves: it is the gift of God."* There are many other Scriptures which confirm that salvation is a gift of God which we receive after repentance from our sins by acceptance through faith in Him alone.

But the Baptism of the Holy Spirit, that mighty enduement of power from on high, is **not** something we "take by faith." It is an experience we are commanded to tarry for until we know we have it. When we have received this great infilling of power, we become like a car, the tank of which has just been filled with fuel. We are then ready for service, and only then are we ready. The trouble is that most of us are trying to take the message of the Gospel to the nations on empty fuel tanks. Is it any wonder that, except for comparatively few occasions, the Gospel has still not been preached in power and with signs following in the uttermost parts of the earth?

Why Tarry in Jerusalem?

Why did Jesus tell His followers to tarry in Jerusalem? Remember, He ascended to Heaven from the Mount of Olives (Acts 1:12). It was therefore the closest city and there was a building there which was available to them for a temporary headquarters. It was important that these followers should not be scattered abroad, which was what would have happened if they had returned to their own homes. Besides, Pentecost, the great Feast of Harvest, one of the great Feasts of Israel (Exodus 23:16), which came at the end of the wheat harvest, was due in only another ten days. Jesus had showed Himself alive after His passion by many infallible proofs for a period of forty days (Acts 1:3). During this time He had taught them things pertaining to the Kingdom of God. Luke mentions some of them in Acts 1:4-8 and Luke 24:15-53. Mark also writes about some of these happenings (Mark 16:15-18). Matthew tells very little (Matthew 28:18-20). And John tells about their meeting with Jesus at Galilee and what happened there (John 21:1-25), besides relating the appearing of Jesus to His disciples while they were still in Jerusalem (John 20:10-31).

Pentecost, which means "fifty," was exactly fifty days after the Passover (when Jesus died). So we know that the disciples would have been close to or in Jerusalem, having returned from Galilee where they first went after the death and resurrection of our Lord. Paul mentions some of His appearances to the church of Corinth (I Corinthians 15:5-8) which no one else mentioned. It is evident that He appeared to Paul after His ascension. *"And last of all he was seen of me also, as of one born out of due time."* (I Corinthians 15:8)

Since then many have seen our resurrected Lord in all parts of the world and He has spoken to them in their languages.

The Feast of Pentecost

All the males of Israel were commanded to appear before the Lord God three times in the year (Exodus 23:17, Deuteronomy 16:16). These three times were:

1. At the Passover (Feast of the Unleavened Bread—Exodus 12:1-51, Exodus 23:15, Leviticus 23:4-8, Deuteronomy 16:1-8. It took place on the fourteenth day of the first month, Abib, also called Nisan).

2. At Pentecost (Feast of the Harvest or Firstfruits, later called the Feast of Weeks and in the New Testament called Pentecost—Leviticus 23:13-22, Deuteronomy 16:9-12. Pentecost was celebrated fifty days after Passover, on the sixth day of the third month, Sinah).

3. At the Feast of Tabernacles (Feast of Ingathering, on the fifteenth to twenty-second days of the seventh month, Ethanim, also known as Tisri—Leviticus 23:39-44, Deuteronomy 16:12-15).

The Lord knew that at Pentecost the Jews would be gathering together in Jerusalem from all of Israel and all the diaspora, and it was important that they should witness the phenomenon so that they could report it when they returned home. We know this is true because when the Holy Spirit did fall on the Day of Pentecost and the multitudes came together, they were confounded because every man heard them speak in his own language, i.e. the language of the country from which they had come, and sixteen different nations are named in Acts

2:9-11. So we know that the Jews had come to Jerusalem for the Feast of Pentecost from at least sixteen different countries. In those Feast days the population of Jerusalem was multiplied many times over. Some believe that as many as one to two million visitors came to Jerusalem during the great feasts. Can you imagine what it was like without the modern hotel and motel facilities? The sanitary conditions alone would have been a great problem, not to mention the need for sleeping accommodations and food for such a multitude! Don't tell me God does not love a good drama. He used the magnetism of the great Feast, with all its meaning, to stage one of the greatest of all historical events: the outpouring of the Holy Spirit and the founding of the New Testament Church. He Himself set the stage for the Passover and Pentecost. And He was right on schedule!

In this same way He will set the stage for the next great event which still has not been fulfilled. This is the one to come of which the Feast of Tabernacles is only the type and shadow. And it will be fulfilled right on schedule. I believe that this will happen very soon. Remember, it was at the Feast of Tabernacles that the Jews expected the Messiah to appear. I have a feeling, they won't be disappointed. Is this the reason the Lord brings so many of His children to Jerusalem for the Feast of Tabernacles year after year?

STUDY QUESTIONS

1. Who promised to send us the Holy Spirit?

2. Give Scriptures for the following ministries of the Holy Spirit:
    a. He reveals truth.
    b. He is the Comforter and Teacher.
    c. He reveals Jesus is the Son of God.
    e. He convicts of sin and its consequences.
    f. He is our Guide.

3. In what way does the work of the Holy Spirit resemble the work of Jesus?

4. Jesus not only promised to send us the Holy Spirit. He also commanded us to receive the Holy Spirit. Give the reference.

5. Why did the Lord choose Jerusalem for the city where He poured out the Holy Ghost?

6. What are the three great Feasts of Israel and when are they?

7. Memorize John 14:16, 17 and Luke 24:49.

8. Read Acts 3 and 4.

CHAPTER THREE

THE HOLY SPIRIT IS THE KEY TO POWER

Up until the outpouring of the Holy Spirit there were only a few individuals in history who experienced the power of God in their lives in so great a magnitude as did the early church. The Old Testament mentions these elect few. We see these "giants of power" as being the prophets and deliverers (judges) of the Old Testament. Let us mention a few.

Othniel: *"And the Spirit of the Lord came upon him, and he judged Israel, and went out to war: and the Lord delivered Chushan-rishathaim king of Mesopotamia into his hand; and his hand prevailed against Chushan-rishathaim. And the land had rest forty years. And Othniel the son of Kenaz died."* (Judges 3:10, 11) It was through the power of the Holy Spirit that Othniel delivered Israel from the oppressor and brought peace to God's people for forty years.

Gideon: *"But the Spirit of the Lord came upon Gideon, and he blew a trumpet; and Abi-ezer was gathered after him."* (Judges 6:34) It was only because of the mighty power of the Holy Spirit upon Gideon that he had such commanding power that at the sound of a trumpet he could summon the Israelites together to stand united and fight against their common enemy. It is the anointing that qualifies an unknown person to suddenly become a powerful leader.

Jephthah: *"Then the Spirit of the Lord came upon Jephthah, and he passed over Gilead, and Manasseh, and passed over Mizpeh of Gilead, and from Mizpeh of Gilead he passed over unto the children of Ammon."* (Judges 11:29) Again we see an insignificant and unloved man singled out by the Holy Spirit to be a mighty deliverer in Israel.

Samson: *"And the Spirit of the Lord came mightily upon* *him, and he rent him as he would have rent a kid, and he had nothing in his hand:...''* (Judges 14:6) There we see clearly that the secret power of Samson was not in anything but the Spirit of God. *"...and the Spirit of the Lord came mightily upon him, and the cords that were upon his arms became as flax that was burnt with fire, and his bands loosed from off his hands. And he found a new jawbone of an ass, and put forth his hand, and took it, and slew a thousand men therewith."* (Judges 15:14, 15)

Besides there was Joseph (Genesis 41:38, 39), Joshua (Numbers 27:18), David (I Samuel 16:13) and others.

The Difference Between the Old Testament Experiences and Those of the New Testament

The difference between the Old Testament experiences and those of the New Testament was that the Holy Spirit "came upon" them, but now He comes to "indwell" us. As it says in Judges 13:25 concerning Samson, *"And the Spirit of the Lord began to move him at times in the camp of Dan between Zorah and Eshtaol."* That is why these Old Testament men could fall away from their great heights in God and miss out so drastically in their personal walk of holiness. We see great comparisons in the lives of the Old Testament heroes and the New Testament ones. Noah, Abraham, Isaac, Jacob, Moses, David, even Elijah (men whom we love) all failed God at one time or another in a shameful way. In the New Testament we see the purity of men like Paul, John, Timothy, James and Peter (after he received the Baptism of the Holy Spirit). They were true princes of the church. That is the work of holiness which the Holy Spirit will do in our lives. If we do not walk in this holiness, it could be that we have had only a temporary "experience" and do not possess a true indwelling of His supreme and excellent Holiness. The time has come for us to take an inventory of Pentecostal

Holiness in our personal lives. In many lives it is only a name and not a day-by-day life. And neither will an outward "show" of rules and regulations ever substitute for the inward purity of a life that is lived in the likeness of the Man from Nazareth. Impurities in our lives will soon cause us to lose our God-given vision, and they "push out" the Holy Spirit, for He will not dwell in an unclean vessel.

The Holy Spirit Gives Us Power to Witness

Acts 1:8, *"But ye shall receive power after that the Holy Ghost is come upon you: and ye shall be witnesses unto me both in Jerusalem, and in all Judea, and in Samaria, and unto the uttermost part of the earth."*

This is one of the most powerful statements ever made by Jesus. *"And when he had spoken these things, while they beheld, he was taken up; and a cloud received him out of their sight."* (Acts 1:9)

It is imperative that we recognize that without the Holy Spirit we can do nothing. Truly, He is the source of our power to be an effective and faithful witness.

Some have drawn our attention to the fact that this word which has been translated "witnesses" comes from the Greek *martus*, which carries the meaning of "martyrdom." To be a true "witness" in those days, and even in some parts of our world today, one has to reckon with the possibility of laying down one's life for the Lord. It is only through the power of the Holy Spirit indwelling us that we can have the strength and courage to suffer and die for the Lord. Without Him we are "born cowards."

This truth is nowhere so obvious as in the life of Peter who, before receiving enduement of power from on high, denied that he knew Jesus. Three times he denied that he knew the Lord (John 18:17, 25, 27). The last time he even cursed (Matthew

26:74), saying, "I know not the man." Yet, after Peter had been filled with the Holy Spirit he became the spokesman for the church, the preacher of Pentecost and one of the foremost leaders. Tradition tells us that he even laid down his life for Christ. That is the difference which the Holy Ghost will make in anyone's life. In a moment of time he was transformed into another person.

Is it any wonder that the early church had the most missionary minded evangelists of all time? The fire of Pentecost burned in their veins, driving them to the uttermost parts of the earth and giving them a supernatural courage which enabled them to do great exploits for God and turn their world upside down (Acts 17:6).

Truly it takes the power of the Holy Spirit to get the job done. This is why Satan has fought this truth so hard. He does not want the world to be evangelized. He wants to continue to drag souls into hell. He knows that a powerless Gospel will never touch the lives of the heathen nor the cultured sinner. It takes the power of the Holy Ghost working in the lives of God's ambassadors with signs and wonders and anointed preaching that is pregnant with power to touch and change the lives of the lost, the rebellious and the hard-hearted.

The Holy Spirit Gives Us a Vision and Burden for Souls

It also takes the infilling of the Holy Spirit in our lives to give us a burden for souls and a vision for missions. Unless the Holy Spirit baptizes us with power from above, we see through carnal eyes. But His Baptism of fire will burn the scales of indifference off our eyes so that we will have a true burden of the Lord and a vision to evangelize. How true that *"Where there is no vision, the people perish... "* (Proverbs 29:18) These words are inscribed in the Parliament Buildings of Canada at Ottawa, Ontario.

Having spent the larger part of my life on the mission field, I can honestly say that it is the lack of vision in the hearts of the church that is responsible for the multitudes who have perished and gone to a Christless grave in the last two millennia of time. And the reason for this lack of vision is our spiritual emptiness. Oh, how we need a fresh and mighty outpouring of the Holy Spirit, an outpouring from on high that will drive us to our knees where we will tarry until we receive!

Tarry for the Holy Spirit in Your Life

We are living in a modern society where we demand speed and instant service. Photos can be developed instantly, dry-cleaning in an hour, speed reading a book in an hour or two, coffee, tea, soups, puddings are concocted "instantly." We even have instant love affairs and divorces. We mock the truth of waiting on God for His power in our lives. So also we have instant "tongues." Sad to say, the fire is missing, the power is missing, the holiness is missing and the signs and wonders are missing, even as the changed lives are missing. Let us face up to it. Our Pentecostal (Charismatic, if you prefer) witness is as shallow as our experience has been because we won't pay the price. We want everything at a bargain rate, and so we have a bargain counter experience. Come, let us reason together! Let us, each of us, face the truth and find our personal Upper Room where we can tarry until the cloven tongues of fire fall upon us. Let us not follow the crowd from shallow experience to shallow experience, but let us break away so that we might experience the depths of Jesus Christ in our lives.

STUDY QUESTIONS

1. Give examples of men in the Old Testament who did great things through the power of the Holy Spirit.

2. What was the difference between the lives of the Old Testament men and the New Testament leaders of the church?

3. What is the true meaning of the word "witness" in Acts 1:8?

4. Who was one of the most transformed men after he was filled with the Holy Spirit?

5. Explain how the Holy Spirit gives us a vision for souls, and what that has to do with world-wide missions.

6. What is the trouble with most of our Pentecostal experiences? Why do they not transform men?

7. Memorize Acts 1:8.

8. Read Acts 5-7.

CHAPTER FOUR

THE BIBLE ACCOUNT OF THE BAPTISM OF THE HOLY SPIRIT

We must go to the Bible for our pattern. Many people have had wonderful experiences that are truly supernatural and of God. But the Book of Acts lays down a clear and distinguishable scriptural pattern which we do well to heed.

The First Outpouring—Acts 2:1-4

"And when the day of Pentecost was fully come, they were all with one accord in one place. And suddenly there came a sound from heaven as of a rushing mighty wind, and it filled all the house where they were sitting. And there appeared unto them cloven tongues like as of fire, and it sat upon each of them. And they were all filled with the Holy Ghost, and began to speak with other tongues, as the Spirit gave them utterance." Three things happened which we must take note of:

A. There came a sound from Heaven of a mighty rushing wind which filled all the house where they were sitting.

B. Cloven tongues of fire suddenly appeared out of nowhere and sat upon each one of them.

C. As they were filled with the Holy Ghost, they began to speak in other tongues—**as the Spirit gave them utterance.**

What it does not say, but is understood, is that there must have been a lot of noise, because a large crowd gathered to see what was happening. Some even mocked and said they were "full of new wine," i.e. intoxicated.

It was then that Peter stood up and preached his first and greatest recorded sermon, proving from the Scripture that this was the fulfillment of the prophecy which had been given to

Joel, confirming the resurrection of Jesus Christ, which was also prophesied by King David. Peter then laid the blame for Jesus' crucifixion on them, *"...God hath made that same Jesus, whom ye have crucified, both Lord and Christ* (the Messiah and Anointed One).*"* And then he called them to repent and be baptized in the Name of Jesus Christ for the remission of sins, promising them that they, too, could receive this same experience of the Baptism of the Holy Spirit. *"For the promise is unto you and to your children and to all that are afar off, even as many as the Lord our God shall call."* (Acts 2:14-39)

There was such Holy Ghost power and anointing on Peter that they were "pricked in their hearts." The Word he preached went like a sword straight to their hearts, convicting them mightily of their sins.

The result was that three thousand souls were swept into the Kingdom of God as they received the Word gladly, and were instantly baptized in the many baptismal baths that stood around the entrance of the Temple. Archeologists have recently discovered them on the south side of the Temple entrance. The worshippers traditionally baptized themselves before they went into the Temple to worship.

Revelation 21:27 (speaking of the New Jerusalem, the eternal Temple of God) says, *"And there shall in no wise enter into it any thing that defileth, neither whatsoever worketh abomination, or maketh a lie: but they which are written in the Lamb's book of life."* The earthly Temple was a pattern of the heavenly one. This explains the ceremonial cleansing which the worshippers observed at the time of Christ. These baptismal fonts were called *Mikvah* in Hebrew.

The Second Outpouring of the Holy Spirit

The second outpouring of the Holy Spirit took place after

the crippled man was healed at the gate of the Temple. Because of the commotion which that miracle caused, Peter and John were arrested by the religious leaders and held for interrogation. After Peter's and John's valiant defence they were released with the command that they were not to speak or preach in the Name of Jesus any more. Peter and John told them they would obey only God. (Acts 4:3-22)

After Peter and John returned to "their own company," they reported what had happened and how they had been threatened by the leaders. This inspired a prayer meeting. And they asked God for greater boldness and for mighty miracles of healing to take place. It was while they were fervently praying that they received another outpouring of the Holy Spirit in their midst. Acts 4:31, *"And when they had prayed, the place was shaken where they were assembled together; and they were all filled with the Holy Ghost, and they spake the word of God with boldness."*

Take note of what happened this time:

A. The place was shaken by the power of God (something which it does not mention the first time).

B. When they were filled with the Holy Ghost, they were anointed to preach with boldness. This is what they had asked God to give them: a new holy boldness (Acts 4:29).

The Third Time the Holy Spirit Was Poured Out

Skipping over the incidents in Samaria because there are no details given (Acts 8:17), let us go on to the next great outpouring of the Holy Spirit which took place under Peter's ministry. Acts 10:1-43 tells us how Peter was called to preach the Gospel for the first time to the Gentiles. Cornelius, a Roman centurion, and his family are solemnly listening to the Gospel story as it falls from the anointed lips of Peter when suddenly something wonderful and totally unexpected takes place. God throws out the format of repentance and baptism, for while Peter yet spake the Holy Ghost fell on all them that heard the Word. The Bible story tells us how astonished the Jewish believers, who had come with Peter, were that such a thing would happen, but they could not deny it, for they heard them speak with tongues and magnify God. Even Peter said, *"Can any man forbid water, that these should not be baptized, which have received the Holy Ghost as well as we?"* (Acts 10:47) And so they were baptized **after** they received the gift of the Holy Ghost. That is how little the New Testament God cares about man-made rituals!

Later Peter in making his defence for his unscheduled "revival" before the church elders in Jerusalem reports, *"And as I began to speak, the Holy Ghost fell on them, as on us at the beginning. Then remembered I the word of the Lord, how that he said, John indeed baptized with water; but ye shall be baptized with the Holy Ghost. Forasmuch then as God gave them the like gift as he did unto us, who believed on the Lord Jesus Christ, what was I, that I could withstand God? When they heard these things, they held their peace, and glorified God, saying, Then hath God also to the Gentiles granted repentance unto life."* (Acts 11:15-18)

Here there was only one supernatural manifestation. There was no fire, no wind, no shaking, no loud noise—only the manifestation of speaking in tongues in the same way as Peter and all the other followers of Jesus had on the Day of Pentecost.

The Fourth Time the Holy Spirit Was Outpoured

The fourth significant outpouring of the Holy Spirit took place under Paul's ministry in Ephesus, *"And it came to pass, that, while Apollos was at Corinth, Paul having passed through the upper coasts came to Ephesus; and finding certain disciples, He said unto them, Have ye received the Holy Ghost since ye believed? And they said unto him, We have not so much as heard whether there be any Holy Ghost. And he said unto them, Unto what then were ye baptized? And they said, Unto John's baptism. Then said Paul, John verily baptized with the baptism of repentance, saying unto the people, that they should believe on him which should come after him, that is, on Christ Jesus. When they heard this, they were baptized in the name of the Lord Jesus. And when Paul had laid his hands upon them, the Holy Ghost came on them; and they spake with tongues, and prophesied. And all the men were about twelve."* (Acts 19:1-7)

This was an unusual case. These twelve disciples apparently had never been baptized in the Name of Jesus. They were a group of godly people who had accepted the teaching of John the Baptist, experienced the baptism of repentance, but had gone no further.

Paul immediately realized that there was something missing in their experience. (This is not difficult, for when you are filled with the Holy Spirit you can usually discern when another Christian is not Spirit-filled.) As soon as Paul taught them the truths of the Gospel through Jesus Christ they were open to receive this truth and be baptized in the Name of the Lord Jesus. *"And when Paul had laid his hands upon them, the Holy Ghost came on them; and they spake with tongues, and prophesied."* (Acts 19:6)

Pause and see what happened. Again, there was no wind nor fire nor shaking accompanying their infilling of the Holy Ghost. But something did happen:

1. They spoke with tongues.
2. They prophesied.

Is this not significant, that in all these outpourings except the second one which seems to have been more of a refilling than an infilling, they all spoke with other tongues? This was a language other than the one they had learned. It was a new language given to them by the Holy Spirit on the instant of their being filled.

It seems therefore from a scriptural standpoint that the one significant and consistent evidence that accompanied all the baptisms of the Holy Spirit in the New Testament was the evidence of speaking in tongues.

What about Paul? In Acts 9:1-31 we read about Paul's conversion in Damascus. The Lord sent the prophet Ananias to pray for him to receive his sight after he had been smitten with blindness on his way to Damascus, *"And the Lord said unto him, Arise and go into the street which is called Straight, and inquire in the house of Judas for one called Saul, of Tarsus: for, behold, he prayeth, And hath seen in a vision a man named Ananias coming in, and putting his hand on him, that he might receive his sight."* (Acts 9:11, 12)

When Ananias arrived, he put his hands on Paul and said, *"...Brother Saul, the Lord, even Jesus, that appeared unto thee in the way as thou camest, hath sent me, that thou mightest receive thy sight, and be filled with the Holy Ghost."* (Acts 9:17)

Saul (his name had still not been changed) was immediately healed and he straightway was baptized. Here we see Ananias laying hands on him for his blindness and also praying for him to receive the Holy Ghost. However, there is no record of Paul being baptized with the Holy Ghost here or in any other of the times when he gives his testimony. Did Paul then speak with tongues?

Yes, he did! In I Corinthians 14:18 he writes to the church in Corinth and says, *"I thank my God, I speak with tongues more than ye all."* So Paul was a tongues-talking preacher, as were all the writers of the New Testament, for almost all of them were either in the Upper Room or bore witness to this experience through their writings. Speaking in tongues was not a foreign or strange experience to the New Testament church. It was the valid evidence of the Baptism and the indwelling of the Holy Spirit in the lives of the believers (Acts 2:4, 10:46, 47, 11:17, 19:6).

STUDY QUESTIONS

1. What signs and wonders accompanied the first outpouring of the Holy Spirit?

2. What happened in Acts 4:31?

3. What happened when Peter preached to the Gentiles in Caesarea?

4. What happened when Paul exhorted, baptized and laid hands on the men in Ephesus?

5. What identical evidence of the Holy Spirit accompanied the majority of these accounts?

6. Did Paul speak with tongues?

7. Memorize Acts 2:1-4.

8. Read Acts 8-10.

CHAPTER FIVE

WHY HAS SATAN FOUGHT THE TRUTH OF THE EXPERIENCE OF SPEAKING IN TONGUES?

Satan has undoubtedly done all he can to discourage people from receiving this wonderful experience. And he has been very successful because he has not used the sinner to fight and argue against this God-given experience, but rather he has used the believers themselves, and therefore he has been very successful, for these believers have often been popular Bible teachers and their opinion carries a lot of weight.

Paul warned the church at Corinth, *"Wherefore, brethren, covet to prophesy, and forbid not to speak with tongues."* (I Corinthians 14:39) And yet many precious believers have literally been thrown out of their churches when they have received the Baptism of the Holy Spirit and borne witness to others that they speak with tongues. Many have suffered great persecution, misunderstanding and rejection for this experience, yet it is a valid, scriptural New Testament experience—a precious gift of the Father which He desires every one of His children to have.

It is strange that nowhere in the New Testament do we find any opposition to it by the early believers. This then must have come into the church when the church began to lose its first love and its power. At that time unbelief and lukewarmness entered the hearts of the church, bringing unbelief, darkness, blindness and sin.

In the middle ages the church was hardly a testimony to the glory of God. There was wicked sin in the lives of many, from the highest to the lowest. There is almost no account of miracles. The Word of God was not preached; instead it was replaced by the doctrines of man which bind and blind the people. Is it any wonder that the truths of salvation by faith, miracles of healing, raising the dead and speaking in tongues (together with all the other gifts of the Holy Spirit) ceased?

The church needed a cleansing. And thank God, the cleansing began through the revelation of the Word of God that came when men died to give the church the Word of God. The Bible was the most banned book, but there was a hunger in the hearts of the people of God to read it, so they read it secretly, even at the risk of great persecution and death. Let me quote from *Banished For Faith*. This is the account as it was recorded by one of my forefathers in Austria over two hundred years ago:

> ...So they took drastic measures to curb and extinguish such religious fires. Consequently, all who were under suspicion of being inspired by the Lutheran teachings were summoned to the parsonage and asked whether they had any forbidden books. If so, they were strictly ordered to surrender them, and whoever had a Bible, New Testament or any Lutheran book was fined a penalty of 12, 18, 20 or 24 gulden, according to the size of the book. This matter became serious and had to be kept secret, as there were also many scoundrels who sneaked about at night and listened at doors and windows so that they could report to the authorities if someone was reading or singing from forbidden books. These homes were then visited and searched. If any books were found, they were confiscated and the owner had to pay a heavy fine. Consequently, the authorities gave strict orders that everyone had to bring his books to the parsonage where they were examined. Those which were not Catholic were confiscated; the others were stamped with a seal and returned. The Church did not accomplish much with this because the people did not bring in all the forbidden books, only the Catholic ones. The Bible and other books were hidden.
>
> This became known to the authorities, who then

searched the homes. If they found a book without the proper stamp or seal, the owner was whipped without mercy and had to pay a heavy fine. The priests and chaplains also preached relentlessly against Martin Luther's teachings and condemned him to hell. One of the priests said, "Nothing remains in order any more and many assume duties for which they are not fitted. The plow, the whip, or the ox-goad belongs in the hands of the farmer or householder, and not the Book. The dipper and pail belong to the housewife, and not the Book. The hoe, the ax, the flail and the manure fork belong to the hired man, and not the Book. The spinning wheel, the feeding of hogs and that kind of work belongs to the maid, and not the Book. Nobody is satisfied anymore with his station in life; all want to be spiritual leaders....Through his messengers or sheriff, the judge summoned all who were under suspicion to appear before him at Spittal for a hearing, and ordered them to recant and return to the Catholic religion. People were threatened and whipped, especially the young people. Many were imprisoned several weeks in order to scare them. Those who remained steadfast and refused to recant were informed that they would not be tolerated and could not remain in the land. They would be driven away from their houses and homes and banished to Siebenbürgen (Transylvania), in present-day Rumania, where Lutheranism was conditionally tolerated. They were warned how they would be treated there and that they would have to live in poverty for the rest of their days. Their small children would die from hunger....

    The end result was that they had to leave Austria. (For more information on how to order *Banished for Faith*, see the back of this book.)

    As God's people came out of darkness, they came out step

by step, truth by truth, revelation by revelation. Slowly the Word of God was restored to the church.
—Repentance of sins by Girolamo Savonarola
—Justification by faith by Martin Luther
—Baptism **after** conversion by the Anabaptists
—Sanctification and a life of holiness by the Wesley Brothers
—Perfect love and death to self by Madame Jeanne Guyon
—A Missionary vision by William Carey
—Healing for the sick by Alexander Dowie
—The Baptism of the Holy Spirit which came spontaneously in wide-spread areas, but surely accompanied the Azusa Street outpouring of the Holy Spirit. Along with all these restored truths came many more. That is what happens when the light is turned on. The darkness of superstition and error must flee away.

The Difference Between the Initial Evidence of Speaking with Tongues and the Gift of Tongues

In I Corinthians 12 Paul writes about the nine gifts of the Spirit. There are more but these are the initial nine. In verse 10 we read, *"...to another divers kinds of tongues..."* What does Paul mean?

I believe there is a definite difference between the initial evidence of speaking with tongues, that accompanies the Baptism of the Holy Spirit, and the gift of tongues. The one who speaks with tongues when he is filled with the Holy Spirit may never be used of the Holy Spirit to give public messages in tongues to the body of the church. He may only use his language as a prayer language in his private prayer time. This is for his own edification (I Corinthians 14:4, *"He that speaketh in an unknown tongue edifieth himself; but he that prophesieth edifieth the church."*) But the "gift of tongues" is for the edification of the church when it is accompanied by interpretation, and is equal to the gift of prophecy. *"...for greater is he that prophesieth than he that speaketh with tongues, except he interpret, that the church may receive edifying."* (I Corinthians 14:5) Satan therefore fights this gift because he does not want the individual believer or the church to be edified. He wants to break man's communion with God, *"For he that speaketh in an unknown tongue speaketh not unto men, but unto God ..."* (I Corinthians 14:2)

The Benefits of Praying in Tongues

1. The Prayer of the Holy Spirit Is Always Prayed in Faith:

Satan works through the minds of men to hinder by using one of the most powerful weapons—unbelief. When we pray in tongues, we cannot intercept our own prayers with unbelief because the spirit prays to God, bypassing the carnal mind, and so the prayer that is offered to God in an unknown language is always prayed in perfect faith, and the prayer that is prayed in perfect faith is always answered. How else can the Holy Spirit pray? He always prays in perfect faith to the Father and cannot be hindered by unbelief.

2. The Prayer of the Holy Spirit Is for the Personal Edification of the Believer (I Corinthians 14:4):

The Spirit of God praying through us searches out our own deepest personal needs—those we don't even recognize ourselves—and intercedes for us to the Father. He tells the Father things that we would seek to hide from God. This is the work of the Faithful Intercessor.

I have heard the Holy Spirit make intercession for the saints through their own mouths in languages which they could not understand but which were known to me. The first time this happened was in Hong Kong. An old Chinese woman who had just arrived in Hong Kong from Communist China was praying in a meeting at which I had been speaking. As I walked among those who had stayed to pray, I heard her praying in perfect English, "Oh God, forgive my great sin, forgive my great sin." I asked one of the elders if he knew her. He told me about her recent arrival. Then to the amazement of both of us we heard her continue to pray this same prayer in English. He said that he knew she positively didn't know a word of English. After the meeting we discovered that she and her son had been gambling on the horses at the Happy Valley Race Track. This was the only thing she had done but it had grieved the Holy Spirit inside of her and He was making intercession for her. Obviously Satan does not want us to confess our sins to the Father, so he will seek to prevent praying in tongues. He well knows most of us are too unrepentant and stubborn and proud to confess our own sins to God.

3. *The Prayer of the Holy Spirit Is Always Prayed in the Will of God:*

Many times we pray for the things which we desire to have or to happen and so we do not pray the Father's will. These are wasted or even sinful prayers. Sometimes God even will give us the desire of our hearts but He will send leanness to our souls (as He did with the children of Israel in the wilderness when they asked for flesh). Psalm 106:15 says, *"And he gave them their request; but sent leanness into their soul."*

It is important that we learn to pray, "Thy will be done," even as Jesus prayed in the Garden and when He taught His disciples how to pray. The longer I live, the more I recognize that this prayer of submission is the highest form of prayer that we can pray. *"And he that searcheth the hearts knoweth what is the mind of the Spirit, because he maketh intercession for the saints according to the will of God."* (Romans 8:27)

This is the prayer of the one who prays with other tongues. He is allowing the Holy Spirit to pray him right into the centre of God's will; and then the Holy Spirit is praying for the person to have the strength to do God's will. This is powerful praying. This is the prayer that is always answered because it is prayed in the will of God. *"And this is the confidence that we have in him, that, if we ask any thing according to his will, he heareth us: And if we know that he hear us, whatsoever we ask, we know that we have the petitions that we desired of him."* (I John 5:14, 15)

4. The Prayer of the Spirit Comes From the Purity of the Spirit.

Sin can hinder our prayers. But the Holy Spirit is without sin, so He has perfect confidence to approach God. He will honestly confess our sins to the Father and instantly break through into the Throne Room on our behalf, for He makes intercession for us. In this way the Spirit of God helps our infirmities, *"Likewise the Spirit also helpeth our infirmities: for we know not what we should pray for as we ought: but the Spirit itself maketh intercession for us with groanings which cannot be uttered."* (Romans 8:26)

When we clearly understand the benefit of praying in the Spirit we can realize why Satan fights this powerful gift so hard. He does not want the church to pull down his strongholds which is what surely will happen when the church begins to pray in the Spirit.

STUDY QUESTIONS

1. Why has Satan fought against speaking in tongues and whom has he used?

2. What warning did Paul give these people in his letter to the Corinthian believers?

3. Explain how the church lost the power of the Holy Spirit.

4. Who were some of God's great leaders God used to restore the truths of the church?

5. What is the difference between the initial evidence of speaking in tongues and the gift of tongues?

6. Give four good reasons why the believer should pray in tongues.

7. Memorize Romans 8:26, 27.

8. Read Acts 11-14.

CHAPTER SIX

HOW DOES SATAN FIGHT SPEAKING IN TONGUES?

Satan is a wiley person. He has had centuries of practice and experience. He knows how to seduce and deceive, especially the children of light. Remember, Eve was a daughter of light when she was deceived. Jesus was right when He said, *"...for the children of this world are in their generation wiser than the children of light."* (Luke 16:8) So Satan will use every plausible argument, often even half-truths, to win his case. And we are gullible enough to fall right into it, all the time thinking we are very wise and making sound, scriptural decisions.

Some of Satan's arguments against speaking in tongues should be reviewed:

1. "The manifestation of speaking in tongues, together with the miracles we read about, stopped after the church was birthed. It was only a passing phenomenon and therefore we should not expect to see miracles or gifts of the Spirit any more. Their use is passed. God doesn't do these things any more. In other words, speaking in tongues is outdated."

And, like Satan did with Jesus, they clearly use the Word of God to prove their point, quoting from I Corinthians 13:8, *"...whether there be tongues, they shall cease ..."*

There is no doubt that all Scripture is inspired, but it must not be taken out of context. In this same verse it also says *"...whether there be knowledge, it shall vanish away."* Now none of those who oppose tongues put these two statements together. We know that knowledge cannot cease until we are translated and then we shall have the eternal revelation of God. All our earthly, carnal man-taught knowledge will be as "ignorance" in comparison to the realm of the all-knowing mind of God, so that this verse is for the future, or at best for another state of existence. We also know that in Heaven there will be no need for speaking in tongues, as all will speak the language of Heaven. Tongues, along with the other gifts of the Spirit—healings, miracles, etc. will not be needed. Yes, this Scripture is valid but as long as we are in the flesh the time for it to be fulfilled has not yet come.

Besides, Peter on the Day of Pentecost clearly said, *"For the promise is unto you, and to your children, and to all that are afar off, even as many as the Lord our God shall call."* (Acts 2:39)

By these words from the most authentic of all New Testament apostles on the subject, the preacher of Pentecost himself, I'm sure we must understand the truth that the gift of the Holy Ghost is for all of God's children.

God has not lost His power, nor Has He changed. Hebrews 13:8 clearly states, *"Jesus Christ the same yesterday, and today, and for ever."* As long as we are in the dispensation of the Holy Spirit we must expect Him to do His office work.

2. *"Those who speak in tongues are fanatics."*

No one likes to be called a fanatic. And yet the world is full of fanatics. There are sports "fans" (which is really only the abbreviation for fanatics). There are also cinema and music (if you can call rock music) fans. But somehow, when you apply the same zeal to the things of God, it does not sound right. I know religious fanaticism can be a dangerous thing. It can be as evil as Satan himself. But the ordinary, God-loving, Bible-believing Christian who believes and practices the whole Word of God, including the truths of Pentecost, should never be termed a fanatic in the derogatory sense of the word. He is simply walking in the steps of Peter and Paul and scores of other New

Testament saints. It is a part of the normal Christian experience.

3. *"Talking in tongues is a false cult."*

I can remember the day in a Christian bookstore when I was looking for a book on false cults. Being a new Christian I wanted to learn truth. The book I held in my hand listed many of the false cults of our day. There weren't so many then as there are now. So maybe out of lack of material to fill the book the last chapter was devoted to the "False Cult of Pentecostalism."

I had just been saved and wonderfully filled with the Holy Spirit. God was so special and real to my heart. As I read the author's opinion, my heart asked, "How many dear ones have been turned from the truth because of the prejudice, blindness and unbelief of those who erred because they know not the Scriptures, nor the power of God (Matthew 22:29)?" If the gift of talking in tongues is a false cult, then the founders of the early church were all mixed up in it.

4. *"Talking in tongues is 'of the devil.'"*

It has always puzzled me to see how Christians can attribute more power, signs and wonders and miracles to the devil than they do to God. Somehow, to them God has become very weak, while the devil is busy doing healings, raising the dead, casting out devils and talking in tongues!! Why are the Christians the first to attribute the works of God to being the works of the devil? The religious people even did it in the days of our Lord. The leaders from Jerusalem said of Him, *"...He hath Beelzebub* (the devil), *and by the prince of devils casteth he out devils."* (Mark 3:22)

Jesus gave them the right answer. *"...How can Satan cast out Satan? And if a kingdom be divided against itself, that kingdom cannot stand."* (Mark 3:23, 24) Satan would never give glory to God by doing miracles in the Name of Jesus.

5. "The whole thing is ridiculous."

Last of all, Satan tries ridicule and mockery to make the wonderful experience appear ridiculous. It is true that the things of God, such as preaching the cross is foolishness to them that perish (I Corinthians 1:18).

On the day of Pentecost the crowds also mocked and said, *"...These men are full of new wine."* (Acts 2:13) Mocking can be very cruel. Hebrews 11:36 calls it "cruel mockings." So if you don't want to appear ridiculous and foolish to the unbeliever (including Christians) then you better not ask God to give you the Baptism of the Holy Spirit with speaking in tongues. There still is a price to pay, and don't you forget it.

Many will deny their experience so that they can climb up in society and be accepted by the masses. But those who are willing to be counted with the 120 of the Upper Room will never be sorry.

STUDY QUESTIONS

1. Who is the real opponent to speaking in tongues?

2. Give five arguments used against the truth of speaking in tongues.

3. Explain I Corinthians 13:8.

4. Why do you believe speaking in tongues is scriptural?

5. Memorize Acts 2:38, 39.

6. Read Acts, chapters 15-17.

CHAPTER SEVEN

SCRIPTURES WHICH REFER TO THE BAPTISM OF THE HOLY SPIRIT

I. Old Testament Scriptures

1. Stammering Lips

Isaiah 28:11: Isaiah prophesied concerning this remarkable experience which was still 600 years to come after his day, *"For with stammering lips and another tongue will he speak to this people."*

How well this describes what happens when the Holy Spirit comes in. Many times the recipient first begins to stammer as the power of God touches the lips, and sounds never before articulated from the organs of speech begin to come forth.

Often it sounds like the first few words of a child learning to speak until the one receiving realizes how easy it is to let go and allow the Holy Spirit to speak through him. Many refuse to take that step of faith and trust because they don't want to appear ridiculous, and so they are always on the edge of receiving but are never fully satisfied.

· Others try to speak their own language and in tongues at the same time. This is impossible. One cannot speak two languages, two words of two different tongues simultaneously. You must give up your own language (your mother tongue) to speak your Father's language.

2. The Promised Rest

Then Isaiah goes on to say, *"...This is the rest wherewith ye may cause the weary to rest; and this is the refreshing ..."* (Isaiah 28:12)

How beautiful this rest really is, only the Spirit-filled saint knows! He can rest in the Lord while the Holy Spirit does the praying and interceding through him. However, Isaiah warns, *"...yet they would not hear."* How sad! The Holy Spirit saw that even as God's own people would reject Jesus, they would, in the same way, reject the Holy Spirit.

Paul repeats this warning Isaiah gave in 28:12 in I Corinthians 14:21, 22, proving that Isaiah was referring to speaking in tongues.

Also the writer of Hebrews speaking of this "rest" in God warns, *"Let us therefore fear, lest, a promise being left us of entering into his rest, any of you should seem to come short of it."* (Hebrews 4:1)

Some of the greatest things God has for us are not acquired by works, but rather by reaching out and receiving them in simple faith and trust.

3. The Pure Language

Zephaniah 3:9 says, *"For then will I turn to the people a pure language, that they may all call upon the name of the Lord, to serve him with one consent."* The wonderful unity (to be of one consent) in prayer and worship that the prophet Zephaniah refers to will only come to pass as we all speak that pure language.

Your own language you yourself have defiled. You have spoken evil against God and man with your language. But when the Lord gives you a new Heaven-sent language, it is pure and clean. It is the language of the Holy Spirit, the tongue of angels (I Corinthians 13:1).

4. Upon All Flesh

One of the greatest prophecies concerning the outpouring of the promised Holy Spirit was given by the prophet Joel. Joel was enabled by God to look across the centuries of time and see the mountain top visitations of God. He saw the outpouring of the Holy Spirit on the day of Pentecost. And he also saw the one to come, which has already begun, but which shall wax greater and greater until it shall culminate in such a great visitation of God that it will be like all the mighty moves of God put together in one great visitation. *"Be glad then, ye children of Zion, and rejoice in the Lord your God: for he hath given you the former rain moderately, and he will cause to come down for you the rain, the former rain, and the latter rain in the first month. And the floors shall be full of wheat, and the vats shall overflow with wine and oil."* (Joel 2:23, 24)

Looking ahead to this mighty outpouring Joel said, *"And it shall come to pass afterward, that I will pour out my Spirit upon all flesh; and your sons and your daughters shall prophesy, your old men shall dream dreams, your young men shall see visions:"* (Joel 2:28, 29)

5. John the Baptist Prophesied Concerning the Baptism of the Holy Spirit

John the Baptist should be included in this list, for he truly was still living in the Old Testament dispensation.

In Matthew 3:11 he said, *"I indeed baptize you with water unto repentance: but he that cometh after me is mightier than I, whose shoes I am not worthy to bear: he shall baptize you with the Holy Ghost, and with fire."*

Jesus referred to this prophecy by John in His last words to His followers when He *"...commanded them that they should not depart from Jerusalem, but wait for the promise of the Father, which, saith he, ye have heard of me. For John truly baptized with water; but ye shall be baptized with the Holy Ghost not many days hence."* (Acts 1:4, 5)

II. New Testament Scriptures That Refer to the Baptism of the Holy Ghost

1. Jesus to the Multitude

Besides the Scriptures we have already mentioned in Chapter Two, Jesus made a very powerful statement concerning the Holy Spirit:

"...Ask, and it shall be given you; seek, and ye shall find; knock, and it shall be opened unto you. For every one that asketh receiveth; and he that seeketh findeth; and to him that knocketh it shall be opened. If a son shall ask bread of any of you that is a father, will he give him a stone? or if he ask a fish, will he for a fish give him a serpent? Or if he shall ask an egg, will he offer him a scorpion? If ye then, being evil, know how to give good gifts unto your children; how much more shall your heavenly Father give the Holy Spirit to them that ask him?" (Luke 11:9-13)

This is a very comforting word, especially for those who are afraid to ask God for the Baptism of the Holy Spirit. To you who have this fear, I would say, read these words of Jesus and don't be afraid. Begin now to start asking and knocking, and do not fear. You will not receive a stone nor a serpent nor a scorpion as the devil would like you to think you would.

2. Jesus to the Woman at the Well

Speaking to the Samaritan woman, Jesus told her some of

the greatest truths. He told her about the living water which He would give to all who would ask for it, *"...If thou knewest the gift of God, and who it is that saith to thee, Give me to drink; thou wouldest have asked of him, and he would have given thee living water....But whosoever drinketh of the water that I shall give him shall never thirst; but the water that I shall give him shall be in him a well of water springing up into everlasting life."* (John 4:10, 14)

Although He did not tell her that this "Living Water" was the Holy Spirit, later in John 7:37-39 this was explained.

3. Jesus at the Last Day of the Feast

"In the last day, that great day of the feast, Jesus stood and cried, saying, If any man thirst, let him come unto me, and drink. He that believeth on me, as the Scripture hath said, out of his belly shall flow rivers of living water. (But this spake he of the Spirit, which they that believe on him should receive: for the Holy Ghost was not yet given; because that Jesus was not yet glorified." (John 7:37-39)

This "last day" was the seventh day of the Feast of Tabernacles, also called the Day of the Great Hosanna. Hosanna means "Save Now." At this time the Hallel (Psalm 113-118) was read. Their succoths were broken down and the branches were shaken. The dried leaves falling off the branches were symbolic that they had shaken off all their sins. They also prayed Messianic prayers at this time. During the succoth prayers are made for rain.

Golden lamps were lit in the court of the women and water was brought by the young priests from the Pool of Siloam to the Tabernacle in golden vessels where it was poured out during a time of great rejoicing with music. Jewish tradition has it that the Messiah would appear at this time. It is symbolic that at this season of the year Jesus would point to Himself as the Giver of the true Living Water.

Jesus said that the Holy Spirit was the Living Water, and here these LIVING WATERS were referred to as the mighty infilling of the Holy Spirit.

Did the woman of Samaria ever get to Jerusalem? Was she one of those women in the Upper Room who received the Baptism of the Holy Spirit? We don't know. But we know that this blessed experience was even available to her, for Jesus Himself said so.

STUDY QUESTIONS

1. Give three Old Testament Scriptures that refer to the Baptism of the Holy Spirit.

2. Explain "stammering lips."

3. In what way is speaking in tongues a rest?

4. Why is your own language not pure?

5. What did John the Baptist say about the Baptism of the Holy Spirit?

6. In what way does Luke 11:9-13 remove our fears concerning this experience?

7. What did Jesus mean when He spoke of "rivers of living water"?

8. Memorize John 7:37-39.

9. Read Acts 18, 19, 20.

CHAPTER EIGHT

HINDRANCES TO RECEIVING THE BAPTISM OF THE HOLY SPIRIT?

1. Unbelief

Many just do not have faith to believe God to give them this experience. They think it is only for preachers or teachers or evangelists or missionaries, but not for them.

2. A False Sense of Unworthiness

Others feel too unworthy. The devil is very good at reminding us of our past sins and weaknesses. He tells us that when we are perfect then we will receive, and not a moment sooner. Let me tell you he is a liar. We do not receive this gift of grace because we are worthy, but rather because we **need** the Holy Spirit in our lives to make us what God wants us to be.

3. Misunderstanding of God's Will

It is easy to put the blame for this on our false teachers, but really we are without reason. As long as we have a Bible and can read what God says about the Holy Spirit, we have no vaild excuse for ignorance. Also so many of God's people have been baptized in the Holy Spirit from all denominations and we have access to their testimonies. Books have been written about this wonderful experience. No one has an excuse for either ignorance or misinterpretation of the Holy Spirit.

4. Sin

Sin can and will hinder us. Therefore we must sincerely and earnestly confess our sins to the Lord. Peter told the people on the day of Pentecost, "Repent ...and ye shall receive the gift of the Holy Ghost."

5. Lack of Desire or Hunger for God

This is perhaps the biggest of all reasons that many do not receive the Baptism, *"...ye have not, because ye ask not."* (James 4:2)

If we would spend as much energy in seeking for the Holy Spirit as we do for earthly things, if we prayed as hard and with as intense a desire for the Baptism of the Holy Spirit as we do for health, wealth, and other passing things, I am convinced that we would be as powerful as the early church. We would soon bring the glory down and see the greatest outpouring of the Holy Spirit known to man.

The church today is full of men who have never been baptized in the Holy Spirit, and what is worse, many of them have absolutely no interest at all in being filled with the Holy Spirit. Much of the reason for this is because there is a lack of constructive teaching and preaching on this subject.

In the Sermon on the Mount Jesus said, *"Blessed are they which do hunger and thirst after righteousness: for they shall be filled."* (Matthew 5:6) Let not the one who is not hungry or thirsty for God think that he shall receive anything from God. We must have a true desire for more of God. The great revivalists of yesterday who were so mightily used of God all sought earnestly for this great enduement of power from above. They spent hours in prayer and tears for the power of God and were greatly rewarded. (See the advertisement for *Deeper Life*

Experiences of Famous Christians in the back of this book.)

Charles G. Finney, who was one of the greatest revivalists of all time, was mightily filled with the Holy Ghost after his conversion, which immediately launched him into preaching the Gospel the very next day although before that time he had never even prayed in public.

The evening in which he was baptized in the Holy Ghost, he came face to face with Jesus Christ and the room was filled with light. Finney said, "He looked at me in such a manner as to break me right down at His feet."

Finney fell down at the feet of Jesus and poured his soul out to Him, weeping like a child. Later he testified, "I received a mighty baptism of the Holy Ghost, without having any expectation or thought that there was such a thing for me."

No one had ever taught Finney this truth, yet God saw his hungry, seeking heart and He gave it to him.

Finney said, "The Holy Ghost descended on me in a manner that seemed to go through me, body and soul. I could feel the impression like a wave of electricity going through and through me. Indeed, it seemed to come in waves and waves of liquid love. It seemed like the very breath of God. I can recollect distinctly that it seemed to fan me, like immense wings. No words can express the wonderful love that was shed abroad in my heart. I wept aloud with joy and love; and I do not know but I should say, I literally bellowed out of the unutterable gushing of my heart! The waves came over me, one after another until, I recollect, I cried out, 'I shall die if these waves continue and pass over me!' I said, 'Lord, I cannot bear any more!' "

From that day on wherever he went, mighty conviction fell upon people. He didn't even have to speak; just his presence caused men to come under the convicting power of the Holy Ghost and they would break down, weeping for their sins.

He refused to preach from written sermons, saying he

believed that it would hinder the Spirit of God, but he spent hours and days in prayer and fasting, with mighty results in his ministry.

Everywhere he went, he experienced mighty revival. At times the power of God fell like a cloud of glory upon him. He ministered in London, England, where between fifteen hundred and two thousand persons were born into the Kingdom of God in one day.

The great revival which took place under his ministry in 1858-1859 was one of the greatest revivals in the history of the world. 100,000 persons were swept into the Kingdom of God and altogether an estimated 500,000 persons professed conversion to Christ under his ministry during his lifetime.

Neither was Finney the only one whose life left a mighty impact upon the world because of the power of the Holy Ghost in their lives which they had received through the Baptism of the Holy Ghost.

STUDY QUESTIONS

1. Give five things that hinder believers from receiving the Baptism of the Holy Spirit.

2. Will we ever receive something from God because we are worthy?

3. Can we really blame our blind leaders who teach against it? Give three reasons.

4. What reason do you give as the greatest hindrance?

5. Why were some men more used of God than others?

6. Memorize Matthew 5:6.

7. Read Acts 21:22, 23.

CHAPTER NINE

PAUL'S INSTRUCTION REGARDING THE HOLY SPIRIT TO THE CHURCH AT CORINTH

Perhaps one of the most misunderstood and misinterpreted chapters in the New Testament is I Corinthians 14 where Paul is writing to the church at Corinth and giving instructions of church conduct and the proper use of the gifts of the Spirit.

First of all, I would like you to read the whole chapter, from verse one to verse forty.

Paul was a sensible man. He appreciated decency and order in the church. He understood the need for discipline and the teaching of the Word of God. The problem with understanding this chapter comes when so-called "teachers" take certain verses out of true context. Many scriptures are only correctly understood and interpreted when the verses before and after it are carefully studied.

In this chapter Paul is speaking about body ministry in the church. He is encouraging the saints to share what God has given them for the people. He is trying to help, not hinder, the workings of the Holy Spirit.

In verses 4, 5, 12, 19, 23, 28, 33 and 34 Paul mentions "the church." That is the body of believers who have met together for the purpose of worship and learning the truths of God.

He is encouraging the saints to claim and exercise the gift of prophecy. He lists it as one of the greatest gifts for the edification of the believers. He says that only one other gift equals it and that is speaking in tongues when it is accompanied by interpretation (verse 5).

This is understandable. Can you imagine Paul arriving at Corinth or Ephesus, or any of the other churches, and standing up before the people and then "ministering" for two to three hours by speaking in tongues? It would be ridiculous; so is the gift of tongues when used to speak to the church (unless it is accompanied by the gift of interpretation).

Tongues are used for two different reasons:

1. To pray to God. This needs no interpretation.

2. To give messages to the church. Then it should be accompanied with the interpretation either by the one who gives the message or someone else who has the gift of interpretation.

Sometimes I have heard individuals burst out in tongues, and there is no interpretation given, even though the leader and the people wait for it. This can sometimes prove embarrassing for all present.

There are three reasons why this could happen:

1. The person who gave the message does not know there is no one present with the gift of interpretation.

2. The person with the gift of interpretation is too shy or fearful to give it.

3. The message may have been only a personal expression of praise and worship to God and doesn't concern the church.

Problems in Connection with Body Ministry

"Body ministry" is the order of a church service where everyone is given the opportunity to say or do something in a meeting.

Sad to say, this freedom can be abused because there often are those well-meaning saints who feel that the church service is "flat" if they don't have any input. They want to be recognized. Some even are exhibitionists with religious spirits who want to draw the attention of people to themselves. This, too, grieves the Holy Spirit. They would do better to enter a stage career, if all they want is to be seen or heard.

Also there are those who seem to have a special "word" in every service. And some more than once. This robs others of the opportunity of exercising their gift of ministry, as the Holy Spirit seems to call for a limitation of messages in each church service (verses 27-29).

Let us be careful to keep balance. Paul says, *"...I will pray with the spirit, and I will pray with the understanding also: I will sing with the spirit, and I will sing with the understanding also."* (I Corinthians 14:15) Both are correct when used at the correct time.

And then Paul mentions the Old Testament scripture by Isaiah, *"...With men of other tongues and other lips will I speak unto this people; and yet for all that will they not hear me, saith the Lord."* (Verse 21) This is quoting from Isaiah 28:11, proving what I have already said in Chapter 7 that the Lord is prophesying through Isaiah that some day His people would speak with tongues.

Paul gives us a vital truth, *"...And the spirits of the prophets are subject to the prophets."* (Verse 32) Many people think they have to instantly do everything they feel inspired to do or they will grieve the Holy Spirit. Some even interrupt anointed preaching to give their "message." A message should never interrupt the truly anointed messenger. It should only confirm what the Holy Spirit has already said through the speaker, or is about to say.

If you truly have a message from God for the church God will give you an opportunity to give it. It will just "fit in" some time during the service.

Sometimes the leader leaves himself wide open for error, confusion and fleshly messages by "waiting" in silence for a few moments for "body ministry." This is something that has more recently become the custom (in the last twenty years). During those "heavy" silences people get fidgety and nervous and soon certain ones (often the wrong ones) feel they must "fill in" the gap with some so-called prophecy which is nothing more than a few words of encouragement or exhortation and which are good but not really Holy Spirit inspired, only "imagination inspired."

Flow along with the meeting and you will save yourself embarrassment and confusion. You will not grieve the Holy Spirit. He has enough power to speak up and be heard.

Remember, the gifts are given for edification of yourself and others. Prophecy is for the whole church, except when used as a word of knowledge to reveal the secrets of a man's heart to cause him to repent (Verse 4 and 22). And tongues are for your personal edification or as a sign to the sinner. When it is accompanied by interpretation it is equal to prophecy.

Don't forget that the Church of Corinth was a new church. It consisted of both Jews who had accepted Jesus as their Messiah and former pagans. They knew nothing about conducting a church service. The women were not educated in the Scriptures and only very few men were. They were ignorant about such things that we take for granted. They knew nothing about an order of service or liturgy or a Holy Ghost anointed meeting. They had so much to learn and Paul was their teacher.

Last of all, Paul warns, *"...forbid not to speak with tongues."* (I Corinthians 14:39) He is referring to the speaking with tongues in the church. Many churches who once were born in the fires of Pentecost with the accompanying manifestations of the gifts of the Holy Spirit have grown cold and formal. Some even are ashamed of the gifts of the Holy Spirit. I heard of one pastor of a Pentecostal church who warned his congregation, "There will be no speaking in tongues during the service. If you want to speak in tongues, go to the basement." When we relegate the Holy Spirit to the basement, we grieve the Holy Spirit by whom we are sealed (Ephesians 4:30). If He withdraws, we have only empty form and ceremony.

Because there has been so-called confusion in some

Pentecostal churches and gatherings, ministers are often afraid to let the members of the congregation minister as the Holy Spirit leads. Therefore, they keep the services very stiff and formal with no one daring even to say "Amen." I believe that if the pastor or leader is truly anointed of the Holy Spirit and endued with Holy Ghost power from on high, he need not be afraid of letting the Holy Ghost work and use people to minister in the church. The same Holy Spirit who works through people will also keep them in divine order when the leadership has the authroity that comes with the true anointing.

STUDY QUESTIONS

1. Who is Paul speaking to in I Corinthians 14?

2. What does Paul say is the greatest gift?

3. When is it equalled?

4. Name two reasons for speaking in tongues.

5. How can it happen that certain messages in tongues given in the church are not interpreted? Give three reasons.

6. Explain about order in the use of the gifts.

7. Explain I Corinthians 14:39 and memorize.

8. Read I Corinthians 12, 13, 14.

CHAPTER TEN

THE NINE FRUITS OF THE HOLY SPIRIT

Many do not understand the difference between the fruit and the gifts of the Holy Spirit. I think that we need to take a brief look at this subject.

Galatians 5:22, 23, *"But the fruit of the Spirit is love, joy, peace, longsuffering, gentleness, goodness, faith, Meekness, temperance: against such there is no law."*

Paul has just been writing about the works of the flesh. They are a repulsive list—adultery, fornication, uncleanness, idolatry, witchcraft, wrath, strife, envy, murders, drunkenness, etc. He is very realistic about those dark evils which have been in the past (and often quite recent past) of the children of God. All these horrible works have once been a part of our lives. But the Blood of Jesus has cleansed us and the Holy Spirit has filled us. So instead of being the servant of evil, bringing darkness and destruction, we have become the messenger of God, bringing light and life wherever we go through the indwelling Holy Spirit.

What a dramatic change! In exchange for these horrible evils which once controlled our emotions and deeds we have these beautiful gifts of the Holy Spirit. I know that whole books could be written about each one of them. In fact, I myself have written a book about love, *Love, the Law of the Angels* which I consider the greatest of all my writings. (See the advertisement in the back of this book.)

Love

Love is the greatest fruit of the Spirit. Paul himself says in I Corinthians 13:13, *"...but the greatest of these is charity."* Love is the source of all good. God is love (I John 4:8). Jesus is the expression of love. The Holy Spirit is a person and He brings with Him His personality, which includes love and all these wonderful "fruit" which Paul lists.

We strive so hard to attain unto these perfections, but we can never be the source of them ourselves. The Holy Spirit is the source, and when He moves into our lives, He brings into us all that He Himself is. That is why, when someone is **filled**, (not touched or blessed, inspired or moved upon, but **filled**) with the Holy Spirit, He has a complete change of character. Old things have passed away and all things have become new (II Corinthians 5:17).

The fruit of the Spirit is the **result** of the Holy Spirit taking full control of a life. These wonderful attributes are not something we "work on" to develop in ourselves. Every good thing that we have or are is only the result of how much He possesses us and controls us.

Many seek to have the Holy Spirit but they never let the Holy Spirit control or have them. And so one sees only periodic manifestations of the fruit of the Spirit in their lives. The rest of the time "self" dominates them. How sad!

We should never seek for the indwelling of the Holy Spirit so that we can have the gifts of power in our lives. That is the wrong motive. In Acts 8:9-24 we read about Simon, a former sorcerer, who coveted the Holy Ghost so that he could have the same power in his life as the apostles had. He even offered money to Peter and John if they would give him this gift. His motives were not pure. He wanted the power of God so that he would be regarded as some great one, which was already his reputation due to the demonic powers which had been working in his life. Peter reprimanded him sharply and warned him that his heart was not right in the sight of God, commanding him to repent. Great fear struck Simon's heart.

Yet many of God's people, sad to say, are not too much

different than Simon. They would rather have the gifts of the Spirit in their lives than the fruit of the Spirit.

The gifts draw attention to man, but the fruit draw attention to God in our lives. There is no exhibitionism in the fruit. There is only the constant, silent witness, hour by hour and day by day. Against such there is no law!

Why is it some of us lose our joy and peace? Could it be because we do not let the Holy Spirit have full control of every instant of our lives?

Faith

Faith is not only a fruit of the Spirit, it is also a gift. And even as love is the key fruit of the Spirit, faith is the key gift of the Spirit. It is the gift which we need to operate all the other eight gifts of the Spirit.

Meekness

Meekness is also another important fruit of the Spirit, especially when one is being used of God in the operation of the gifts of the Spirit. For soon, because of the adulation one receives from the crowd, due to the miracles seen in the gifted person's life, it is possible to become proud and "lifted up." Yes, it is possible to have the gifts of miracles and healings and still become an outcast. Jesus Himself warned against this in Matthew 7:21-23, *"Not every one that saith unto me, Lord, Lord, shall enter into the kingdom of heaven; but he that doeth the will of my Father which is in heaven. Many will say to me in that day, Lord, Lord, have we not prophesied in thy name? and in thy name have cast out devils? and in thy name done many wonderful works? And then will I profess unto them, I never knew you: depart from me, ye that work iniquity."* Therefore meekness is a very important fruit of the Spirit. The more God uses you, the more important it is to seek for true meekness.

Longsuffering

Without longsuffering how can we have the patience we need to deal with the different situations that come up in the life of the one who is in a place of prominence and responsibility. The more there is required of us, the more we have need of longsuffering and patience. The more closely a person walks with God, the more he observes and is repelled by sin, not only in his own life, but in the lives of others. This is when the fruit of longsuffering is needed, so that we will have patience to wait for God to perfect that other person. We need as much longsuffering for others as we have for ourselves.

Joy

This is one of the most vibrant attractions to Christ. A miserable and unhappy person will never attract you to God. God would have turned this world to Christ hundreds of years ago if only he had had happy, joyous saints. Satan knows this. That is why he has deceived the church into believing that a sad, suffering, unhappy, long-faced person is more spiritual than the joyous one. May the Lord help us to see the truth. Be happy! Let the King rejoice in you!

Goodness

Are not good people a delight! The heart that is kind always thinks of others. It does not seek for self. It is always giving and sharing and blessing others. In a selfish, greedy world the one who has the fruit of goodness will stand out like a beacon light for he always will have time to help and minister to others. Oh God, give us men of goodness!

Peace

What a stormy, turbulent world we live in! How little of peace we have in this world! And yet how hard we strive for it. We have never had so many ambassadors of peace and so little peace. Terrorism, crime, divorce, separations, strife in families, communities, nations and hearts rob us all of peace. Could it be that the reason for it all is because we have forsaken the Prince of Peace? After all, He alone is the giver of peace. And until His Holy Spirit fills us and our lives, we can never have true peace. I know that when our hearts are at peace with God we can have that sweet peace that passes all understanding in our hearts, for that is the promise God gives us through Paul in his letter to the Philippians (Philippians 4:7).

Gentleness

What a wonderful attribute in a rude and aggressive world! Where does one find gentleness in a modern world? Does one only find it in the face of a young baby or an old saint? Where are the "gentle" maidens of yesterday? Surely Jesus was the picture of gentleness when He took the children on His knee and blessed them or when He softly spoke to Mary Magdalene at the tomb after His resurrection. And even when He turned and looked at Peter after Peter had denied Him three times. May the Lord bathe us with gentleness!

Temperance

Is our lack of temperance the reason why we swing from

one extreme to another? I believe it is one of the causes of drunkenness, adultery, violence, obesity, cults and all kinds of extreme fanaticism and way-out fashions. But one of the saddest things that a lack of temperance causes is a tendency to follow all kinds of erroneous teachings. We swing from one extreme to another. This causes cults to be born over night. Error flourishes in the seed-bed of intemperance and gives birth to all kinds of extremism. The true church of God is a well-balanced church, and the true saint of God is as poised as a stately queen.

STUDY QUESTIONS

1. List the nine fruit of the Spirit from Galatians 5:22, 23.

2. Describe briefly the three you think are the most important.

3. What is the most important—the fruit of the Spirit or the gifts of the Spirit?

4. What does the lack of temperance lead to?

5. Memorize Galatians 5:22, 23.

6. Read Acts 24:25, 26.

CHAPTER ELEVEN

THE NINE GIFTS OF THE SPIRIT

Paul lists nine gifts of the Spirit in I Corinthians 12:8-11. He begins this chapter with the word, *"Now concerning spiritual gifts, brethren, I would not have you ignorant."*

God does not want us to be ignorant about the things of God. It is so sad to see Christians who are totally ignorant about the Bible and spiritual things. Someday we will be very sorry for wasting a lifetime of opportunities for gaining spiritual wisdom and knowledge, all because we had no interest in them even though they concern our eternal wisdom, knowledge and welfare.

Pauls says:

1. There are different gifts but the same Spirit.

2. There are different ways of administering these gifts but the same Lord blesses and uses all the different ways.

3. There are different operations, aspects of the gifts, but God works through each different aspect.

So, although they are called "gifts of the Spirit," still we must understand that the Holy Trinity co-operates together to make them possible. And they are given for our spiritual profit.

The gifts of the Spirit are divided into three different categories:

A. Gifts of revelation:
    1. The word of wisdom
    2. The word of knowledge
    3. The discerning of spirits.

B. Gifts of miracles:
   1. The gift of faith
   2. The gift of healing
   3. The working of miracles.

C. Gifts of utterance:
   1. The gift of prophecy
   2. The gift of tongues (diverse kinds)
   3. The gift of interpretation of tongues.

The Holy Spirit chooses to whom He wishes to impart these gifts. Some people have more than one gift. Often it seems that when the Lord sees that someone uses the gift or gifts which He has given that one, in a wise and grateful way, He gives that same person even more gifts. The parable of the talents would imply this same fact (Matthew 25:14-30).

The Lord is that "man" who has "travelled into a far country." But before He left, He called His servants unto Himself and "delivered unto them his goods." (Matthew 25:14). Remember what He said; *"Verily, verily, I say unto you, He that believeth on me, the works that I do shall he do also; and greater works than these shall he do; because I go unto my Father."* (John 14:12) Truly Jesus "delivered unto us His goods." We are responsible for what we do with these precious gifts.

The early church received this same challenge, opportunity and responsibility. That is what the call is all about.

"And these signs shall follow them that believe; In my name shall they speak with new tongues; They shall take up serpents; and if they drink any deadly thing, it shall not hurt them; they shall lay hands on the sick, and they shall recover." (Mark 16:17, 18) This call is not only to the apostles but to "all them that believe." Speaking in tongues and the other miracle gifts are signs that Jesus promised would follow

"the believer," not only the apostle or pastor or missionary, etc.

Verse 20 of this same chapter says, *"And they went forth, and preached every where, the Lord working with them, and **confirming the word with signs following**. Amen."* (See the advertisement for *With Signs Following* at the back of this book.)

In Acts 8:1-4 and Acts 11:19-21 we read that, because of the great persecution, the believers were scattered abroad and they went forth preaching and bearing witness, *"And the hand of the Lord was with them: and a great number believed, and turned unto the Lord."* (Acts 11:21)

The early church went out in the power of the Holy Spirit and did His mighty works because they expected to.

Even before Pentecost, when Jesus sent forth His disciples two by two, He said unto them, *"Heal the sick, cleanse the lepers, raise the dead, cast out devils: freely ye have received, freely give."* (Matthew 10:8)

And again, when Jesus sent out the "seventy," He commanded them, *"And heal the sick that are therein* (the cities), *and say unto them, The kingdom of God is come nigh unto you ..."* (Luke 10:9). *"And the seventy returned again with joy, saying, Lord, even the devils are subject unto us through thy name."* (Luke 10:17)

"Through Thy Name." That was the key. Peter and John commanded the lame man to rise up and walk in the Name of Jesus (Acts 3:6). Later, as they were being questioned and interrogated by the religious leaders, they said, *"Be it known unto you all, and to all the people of Israel, that by the name of Jesus Christ of Nazareth, whom ye crucified, whom God raised from the dead, even by him doth this man stand here before you whole."* (Acts 4:10)

It was "in the name of Jesus" that Paul commanded the demon spirits to come out of the young fortune teller in Philippi (Acts 16:18). And he (the soothsaying demon) came out immediately.

But it is not enough to use the formula. One must have the power of the Holy Spirit in one's life. In Acts 19:13-16 we read how certain men who were not filled with the Holy Ghost tried to cast demons out of a man who was possessed. The men who tried to do this miracle in the Name of Jesus were seven sons of a priest (all Jews). They commanded the demons, *"...We adjure you by Jesus whom Paul preacheth...."* But they didn't get very far, for the evil spirit answered them and said, *"...Jesus I know, and Paul I know; but who are ye?...* (Verse 15) *"And the man in whom the evil spirit was leaped on them, and overcame them, and prevailed against them, so that they fled out of that house naked and wounded."* (Verse 16)

These men had never been filled with the Holy Ghost. They were not even believers. They did not have the authority of God behind them. As we go forth to do the works of God, we **must** have the credentials of the Holy Ghost.

Let us look briefly at these nine gifts of the Spirit. They are all of the same value. Each one is precious.

A. The Gifts of Revelation

1. The Word of Wisdom

This is the gift of "knowing by the Spirit," and not only by learning through experience, the correct and wise decision to make at certain times. It is closely intwined with the word of knowledge and discerning of spirits. It also works closely with the gift of prophecy and interpretation of tongues. The word of wisdom can look into the past and into the future, as well as the present. This is one of the most precious gifts. It operates with anointed preaching and teaching. When it speaks, it carries the authority of Heaven behind it, because it has the wisdom of the sages and the knowledge of Heaven.

2. The Word of Knowledge

This, as I said, is linked with the above, but it is also the ability to see into the heart of a person and know what is taking place. Peter had this gift of knowledge when he "knew" that Ananias and Sapphira were lying and cheating about their love offering (Acts 5:1-11). And then he had the word of wisdom how to handle the affair. It is not enough to have the word of knowledge. We can do harm with any one of the gifts of revelation if we don't use them wisely. The gift of wisdom is one of the most lacking of all gifts in the church.

3. The Discerning of Spirits

This gift enables one to call out the name of an evil spirit and cast it out. Jesus used this gift when He came down from the Mount of Transfiguration and found His disciples trying unsuccessfully to deliver a boy from a very violent spirit. Jesus immediately rebuked the foul spirit, saying unto him, *"...Thou dumb and deaf spirit, I charge thee, come out of him, and enter no more into him."* (Mark 9:14-29) He did not need to ask the demons for information. He refused to converse with them. In fact, He very seldom allowed them to speak (Mark 1:34) nor did He carry on a conversation with them. He knew they were liars. We can get wrong information from the evil spirits if we communicate with them. The gift of discerning of spirits is necessary when casting out demons.

B. The Gifts of Miracles

1. The Gift of Faith

As I mentioned earlier, faith is both a fruit of the spirit and a gift. It is the result of the Spirit-filled life. But it also is necessary to enable one to operate any of the other eight gifts of the Spirit.

This gift of faith is not something you "work up" or "convince your mind by determination" that you will have. It is that sudden "knowing" down inside of you that you already have the miracle even before there is any evidence of it. The Holy Spirit is the sole inspiration of the gift of faith. Smith Wigglesworth of modern times was rightly called "The Apostle of Faith." (See the advertisement for Smith Wigglesworth's books in the back of this book.)

2. *Gift of Healing*

It seems that some are more gifted in healing one kind of sickness than others. Perhaps it is because they have themselves been healed of a certain illness and therefore have more faith for God to heal this particular illness. Let each one of us operate in the capacity of our enablings.

The fruit of the Spirit, such as love, longsuffering, goodness, must accompany the gift of healing. It was with a heart of compassion that Jesus ministered for long hours just healing the sick. It takes hours to pray for long lines of sick people, and many do not have either the love and compassion nor the patience for it.

"And Jesus went forth, and saw a great multitude, and was moved with compassion toward them, and he healed their sick." (Matthew 14:14)

Do not ask God to give you the gifts of healing if you are not willing to stand for hours, day after day, ministering to the sick and suffering, because you will be severely judged if you do not use the "talents" the Holy Spirit has given you.

3. The Working of Miracles

Jesus had this gift in operation when He walked on the water, fed the five thousand and three thousand, raised the dead and suddenly disappeared from the crowd.

Moses had this gift when he divided the Red Sea, brought water from the rock and daily fed the Children of Israel with manna from Heaven.

Elijah also had this gift when he held back the rain for three years, brought it out of the sky and called fire down from Heaven. We claim our God is the God of Miracles, yet we limit our faith to only miracles of healing and finances. Let us launch out into the deep and let down the net. I believe God will give us a "miracle draught of fishes." These are the days when God will do miracles like He did for Peter (deliverance from prison twice). I call Peter the greatest "prison escapee" of all times.

And Paul and Silas also experienced an earthquake and deliverance from prison. Miracles come when we need supernatural deliverances. Maybe one reason we don't have them is because we are not risking great things for God!

C. The Gifts of Utterance

1. The Gift of Prophecy

This is one of the great gifts of the Spirit because it is the gift which speaks forth the oracle of God. Much of the Old Testament, especially the major and minor prophets, are the result of men of God operating under the unction of this gift. They shook nations, were loved and hated. Jeremiah expressed it perfectly when he said, *"Then the Lord put forth his hand, and touched my mouth. And the Lord said unto me, Behold, I have put my words in thy mouth. See, I have this day set thee over the nations and over the kingdoms, to root out, and to pull down, and to destroy, and to throw down, to build, and to plant."* (Jeremiah 1:9, 10) That is the work and ministry of a true prophet.

It is not always easy to give the Word of the Lord in prophecy. God does not always speak in a positive way. He sometimes gives His people a message of correction and rebuke which is hard for them to accept, and so they become angry and hate the prophet. He must be prepared to suffer for the Lord.

There were both men and women in the Old Testament and New Testament whom God called prophets (prophetesses). They operated in this anointing.

Age made no difference. Samuel was a prophet from his childhood. God let none of his words fall to the ground (I Samuel 3:19). *"And all Israel from Dan even to Beer-sheba knew that Samuel was established to be a prophet of the Lord. And the Lord appeared again in Shiloh: for the Lord revealed himself to Samuel in Shiloh by the word of the Lord."* (I Samuel 3:20, 21)

If the prophet is going to be God's messenger, he must live close to God and keep his heart pure before the Lord. He must be ready to lay down his life for the message he has to bring. He will not always only prophesy good things. And all that he prophesies will surely come to pass (Deuteronomy 18:22). If it doesn't, then he is not a true prophet.

We never know whom God will call to be a prophet. The prophet Amos said, *"...I was no prophet, neither was I a prophet's son; but I was a herdman, and a gatherer of sycamore fruit: And the Lord took me as I followed the flock, and the Lord said unto me, Go, prophesy unto my people Israel."* (Amos 7:14, 15)

Not everyone who gives a prophecy now and then is a prophet. The Spirit of God may move on some to give an occasional word of prophecy and that is good, but it does not mean that he is a prophet. A prophet must constantly operate in that capacity.

In the last days we should expect to see God raise up many people who will have the anointing to prophesy. *"And it shall come to pass in the last days, saith God, I will pour out of my Spirit upon all flesh: and your sons and your daughters shall prophesy, and your young men shall see visions, and your old men shall dream dreams: And on my servants and on my handmaidens I will pour out in those days of my Spirit; and they shall prophesy."* (Acts 2:17, 18)

Let God use you in this gift if He desires, and do not be afraid.

2. The Gift of Tongues

Not everyone who is filled with the Holy Spirit has the gift of tongues, even though they had the evidence of speaking in tongues at the time when they were baptized in the Holy Ghost. The gift of tongues is primarily used in giving messages in tongues in the church. It is sometimes hard to understand the purpose for giving a message in tongues when it cannot be understood. But it does have a purpose or the Lord would not have given this gift.

First of all, it is like the sounding of a trumpet. It calls the congregation to a state of alertness. They listen to hear what the Lord is going to say when the interpretation is given.

Second, it is for a sign to the unbeliever (I Corinthians 14:22). This is such a supernatural manifestation (especially when they understand the language, which often happens) that they know God has spoken. This is what happened in the day of Pentecost. *"...we do hear them speak in our tongues the wonderful works of God."* (Acts 2:11)

The wonderful works of God is indeed what people often

are talking about when they speak in tongues as they worship. But when a message in tongues is given the subject is more than words of praise.

Then, of course, the gift of tongues is given for the purpose of intercessory prayer when the Spirit of God prays through us bypassing the mind, and deep calleth unto deep.

The one who has the gift of tongues should ask God to give him the gift of interpretation also (I Corinthians 14:13).

3. The Gift of Interpretation of Tongues

This gift is very similar to the gift of prophecy, and often the one who has the one gift also has the other. This is a very important gift—even equal to prophecy. It gives the gift of tongues credibility. It carries a great impact. It must be operated in perfect faith, for it could be a terrible embarrassment if one were to give the interpretation only to find out later that the message in tongues which preceded it was understood by someone in the church and this so-called "interpretation" is not the correct one. Knowing there is this possibility, the exercising of this gift demands faith on the part of the one who gives the interpretation.

It is one of the most lacking gifts in the church. I pray that God will raise up more people with this great gift. Too many churches do not have anyone who has the gift of interpretation of tongues, and so, after a message in tongues is given, there is no interpretation, and this should not be in a church full of Spirit-filled believers. In fact, it incapacitates the one who has the gift of tongues because he is not permitted to use his gift if there is no one to interpret it. *"But if there be no interpreter, let him keep silence in the church; and let him speak to himself, and to God."* (I Corinthians 14:28)

Let us respect and honour these nine gifts of the Spirit.

The church is weak today because it lacks in these gifts of the Holy Spirit, and the reason it lacks is because it is a church that has rejected the truth of the Baptism of the Holy Spirit.

STUDY QUESTIONS

1. Where do the gifts of the Spirit originate?

2. What are the three different categories of the gifts of the Spirit?

3. List the gifts under each of the above categories.

4. How does Matthew 25:14-30 apply to the gifts of the Spirit?

5. Explain John 14:12. How does it refer to the gifts of the Spirit?

6. In what way is the Name of Jesus connected with the demonstration of the gifts of the Spirit?

7. What do you think are the three most important gifts of the Spirit? Explain.

8. Memorize Mark 16:17, 18.

9. Read Acts 27, 28.

CHAPTER TWELVE

QUESTIONS AND ANSWERS

1. Is the Holy Spirit a Person?

The third Person of the Trinity most certainly is a person. A person is a living being who has a distinctive personality. He (as He is termed, though He has no gender) has emotions like any one of us.

We are limited in understanding because we are limited in experience. We know so little of the spirit-world. Just because the Holy Spirit has no body like we mortals do, it is hard for us to visualize Him with our limited knowledge. But He is a person who portrays the Father God to us in spirit form even as Jesus Christ portrayed the Father God to us in human form. We could see Jesus. Even now He has a body, a glorified, resurrected body. He is easy for us to understand, but the Holy Spirit is only revealed to us by the Spirit Himself.

The Personality of the Holy Spirit

1. He can be vexed by man and so angered that instead of being our "Comforter," He can become our enemy.
Isaiah 63:10, *"But they rebelled, and vexed his Holy Spirit: therefore he was turned to be their enemy, and he fought against them."*

2. He can be grieved.
Ephesians 4:30, *"And grieve not the Holy Spirit of God, whereby ye are sealed unto the day of redemption."*

3. The Holy Ghost speaks.

Mark 13:11, *"But when they shall lead you, and deliver you up, take no thought beforehand what ye shall speak, neither do ye premeditate: but whatsoever shall be given you in that hour, that speak ye: for it is not ye that speak, but the Holy Ghost."*

4. The Holy Ghost teaches.
Luke 12:12, *"For the Holy Ghost shall teach you in the same hour what ye ought to say."*
These last two verses refer to the word of wisdom and the word of knowledge which the Holy Ghost gives in an hour of emergency and urgency.

5. The Holy Ghost calls out people to serve God.
Acts 13:2 and 4, *"As they ministered to the Lord, and fasted, the Holy Ghost said, Separate me Barnabas and Saul for the work whereunto I have called them....So they, being sent forth by the Holy Ghost, departed...."*

6. The Holy Ghost must give us permission to preach.
Acts 16:6, 7, *"Now when they had gone throughout Phrygia and the region of Galatia, and were forbidden of the Holy Ghost to preach the word in Asia, After they were come to Mysia, they assayed to go into Bithynia: but the Spirit suffered* (permitted) *them not."*

7. The Holy Spirit warns of dangers and persecution we will face.
Acts 20:23, *"Save that the Holy Ghost witnesseth in every city, saying that bonds and afflictions abide me."*

8. The Holy Spirit chooses out those who are the spiritual leaders.
Acts 20:28, *"Take heed therefore unto yourselves, and to*

all the flock, over the which the Holy Ghost hath made you overseers, to feed the church of God, which he hath purchased with his own blood."

9. The Holy Ghost is the source of our ability to love.
Romans 5:5, *"And hope maketh not ashamed; because the love of God is shed abroad in our hearts by the Holy Ghost which is given unto us."*

10. The Holy Ghost is the source of our joy.
Romans 14:17, *"For the kingdom of God is not meat and drink; but righteousness, and peace, and joy in the Holy Ghost."*

11. The Holy Ghost gives us hope.
Romans 15:13, *"Now the God of hope fill you with all joy and peace in believing, that ye may abound in hope, through the power of the Holy Ghost."*

12. We live a sanctified life through the power of the Holy Ghost.
Romans 15:16, *"That I should be the minister of Jesus Christ to the Gentiles, ministering the gospel of God, that the offering up of the Gentiles might be acceptable, being sanctified by the Holy Ghost."*

2. What Is the Difference Between the Holy Spirit and the Holy Ghost?

There is no difference. The Holy Spirit of the Old Testament is the same Person as the Holy Ghost. The two different translations are the same person—a ghost is a spirit, a spirit is a ghost.

3. Did the Holy Spirit Ever Fill People in the Old Testament?

That terminology was not used in the Old Testament in the same way as in the church age. As I explained in Chapter Two, in the Old Covenant the Holy Spirit "came upon" the people of God at times.

They certainly had wonderful experiences of the infilling of the Holy Spirit, for example:

Luke 1:15: John the Baptist was filled with the Spirit from his mother's womb.

Luke 1:41: Elizabeth was filled with the Holy Spirit and prophesied.

Luke 1:67: Zacharias was filled with the Holy Spirit and prophesied.

Luke 1:35: Mary was told by the angel Gabriel that *"...The Holy Ghost shall come upon thee, and the power of the Highest shall overshadow thee: therefore also that holy thing which shall be born of thee shall be called the Son of God."* Although these Scriptures are in the New Testament, the characters were living in the Old Testament dispensation.

The Baptism of the Holy Spirit is a gift of God to endue with power from on high all who believe (not only the Johns, Elizabeths, Marys, etc.). The accompanying gifts are for the purpose of witnessing with power the Gospel of Christ to the whole world.

4. Does Everyone Who Is Filled with the Holy Spirit Speak with Tongues?

It seems from the accounts given in Acts 2:4, 10:46 and 19:6 that speaking with tongues is the initial evidence of the New Testament experience of the Baptism of the Holy Spirit.

The Holy Spirit speaks His own language when He comes in. He is not dumb. Don't settle for less!

5. Does One Receive the Baptism of the Holy Spirit at Conversion, Baptism or Confirmation?

It is possible to be saved and filled with the Holy Spirit at the same time, but they are definitely two separate works of grace in the life. Neither does one automatically receive the Holy Spirit at baptism (whether infant or otherwise), nor confirmation, though one can be filled with the Holy Spirit when being baptized or confirmed (after conversion), but again, it is a separate work of grace.

6. Is It Necessary to Lay Hands on a Person for Him to Receive the Holy Spirit?

No! The laying on of hands can be a point of contact for the one who has difficulty in believing. It helps his faith and it is scriptural. Paul laid hands on the men in Ephesus when they received (Acts 19:6), but it is not necessary. Neither on Pentecost, nor in the house of Cornelius were hands laid on the believers when they received. The laying on of hands is for another purpose. One can receive the Holy Spirit while praying alone.

7. Can One Be Baptized in the Holy Ghost More Than Once?

There is only one original Baptism of the Holy Spirit, but there are many refillings. Paul writes to Titus (Titus 3:5) about the "renewing of the Holy Ghost." Many who once were anointed have grown cold in their soul and lost that anointing.

They need to repent and ask the Lord for a fresh anointing and infilling. We all need to be renewed in the Holy Ghost day by day.

8. What Qualifications Must One Have to Be Baptized With the Holy Ghost?

Peter put it clearly and simply, *"...Repent, and be baptized every one of you in the name of Jesus Christ for the remission of sins, and ye shall receive the gift of the Holy Ghost. For the promise is unto you, and to your children, and to all that are afar off, even as many as the Lord our God shall call."* (Acts 2:38, 39)

This blessed experience is for every one of God's children. You do not have to try to "make yourself perfect" before God can fill you. The Holy Spirit will clean you up on the inside as He comes in. He is like a mighty river of cleansing. It is a gift of God given in answer to Jesus' prayer to the Father, *"And I will pray the Father, and he shall give you another comforter, that he may abide with you for ever; Even the Spirit of truth; whom the world cannot receive, because it seeth him not, neither knoweth him: but ye know him; for he dwelleth with you, and shall be in you."* (John 14:16, 17)

9. Can One Be "Taught" How to Speak in Tongues?

How can you teach the Holy Spirit how to speak in tongues? Never. When He comes in He will speak of His own accord, using our mouths.

Unfortunately, some try to "teach others how to speak in tongues." I have heard some even tell the seeker, "Say ba-ba—that's it! Now you are speaking in tongues."

This is a farce. The poor seeker goes away trying to believe that he has received, but there is no evidence and no power in the life. I want to warn you, don't seek for gifts, seek the Giver. He has the gifts.

10. Can the Devil Speak in Tongues?

Yes! I have heard him use demon possessed people whom he has spoken through. But this should not discourage the true believer from seeking for the promise of the Father. Those I heard speak were demon possessed or devil worshippers. Remember Satan always copies God.

11. Is Tongues an Earthly Language or a Heavenly One?

I believe it can be both. I have heard languages I could understand. And I myself have spoken in tongues and been understood—Korean, a language I never learned and didn't even know I was speaking until it was told me later.

I Corinthians 13:1 mentions the "tongue of angels." This could be the heavenly language.

12. What Did John the Baptist Mean by the Holy Ghost and Fire?

Matthew 3:11, *"I indeed baptize you with water unto repentance: but he that cometh after me is mightier than I, whose shoes I am not worthy to bear: he shall baptize you with the Holy Ghost, and with fire."*

The fire of God always speaks of purging and cleansing. John was baptizing in the Jordan. Water baptism is an outward expression of an inward experience. It was a sign of a work of repentance and cleansing in the heart. It is an act of man.

The baptism of fire is not an act of man; it is a mighty work of the Holy Ghost. He comes like a fire into the innermost depth of our lives and burns out the dross and the tin, doing a mighty work of grace in our lives that changes our whole character, and makes room for Him to come and live His life in and through us, for our God truly is a mighty consuming fire. (Deuteronomy 4:24, Hebrews 12:29)

CONCLUSION

In a Bible study of this size it is impossible to answer everyone's questions about the Baptism of the Holy Spirit. And even if every question anyone has ever had would be answered, still, only the Holy Spirit can convince one that the teachings of this study are the truths of God.

This subject is so sacred that I have always refused to debate or argue it with anyone. I believe that the Holy Spirit Himself will reveal these truths to any sincere and honest seeker who really wants to know the truths concerning the Holy Spirit, if he will humbly ask God to help him.

Go to God with an open mind, confessing:
1. Your need and hunger for God,
2. Your powerless life,
3. Your sins, failures and fears,

and He will surely give you the precious Baptism of the Holy Spirit.

This is a wonderful experience, and God is more ready to give than we are to receive. We do not need to understand everything about the Holy Spirit in order to receive this great gift of God. We do not understand electricity, but we accept and are grateful for the manifold benefits we receive from it.

I remember how that, after my conversion, I wanted all that God had for me. I loved Jesus so much and I was really trying to obey Him and be His faithful follower to serve Him. Yet, in spite of this true desire in my heart, the last thing I wanted was to be "filled with the Holy Spirit—and speak in tongues like those 'crazy Pentecostals' did!" I even voiced this opinion very strongly.

But God, who knew what I really wanted (because He knew my heart) and realized that I was ignorant of His goodness, disregarded my opinions, for He knew they were based on ignorance and prejudice.

One month later, while in prayer, God gave me a mighty anointing of power. It was so wonderful that I felt I was a new creature. It was all glory, glory, glory! I felt like I was in Heaven. When a sister, who was praying with me, saw what had happened to me said, "Gwen, you almost received the Baptism of the Holy Spirit tonight!" I was so amazed. I asked her, "Is this what the Baptism of the Holy Spirit is like?"

She answered, "Of course, it's the same, only you will speak in tongues when you are filled."

Then I knew of a certainty that:

1. it was real,
2. it was of God (the devil could never give me this glory),
3. I wanted it,
4. I needed it, for I soon found myself powerless to witness for Christ.

Three months later, while praying for an unsaved member of my family, God mightily filled me with the Holy Ghost. The power of God was so mighty upon me that I felt as though I was being translated.

I cried and laughed and shouted and praised God until long past midnight in the heavenly language which the Holy Spirit gave me as He filled me with the glory and power of God. It was so wonderful that I can remember feeling as though I was standing in the very presence of the Lord. In fact, it was as though I was in Heaven and not upon this world any more. I believe that we are given the gift of tongues because the physical body is not able to contain or express the magnificent majesty and magnitude of the glory of God. For then the Holy Ghost breaks through the boundaries of our human and frail limitations, and He praises and extols the Lord of glory in a language superseding our mental or oratorial abilities and befitting His great excellence.

This wonderful, heavenly experience lasted from about 9 p.m. until past midnight. It took place in my bedroom in the home where I lived with my parents. The windows were open but I didn't care if the whole world heard me praising God, for now not only were the windows of my room opened, my heart had been opened and enlarged to a new dimension and revelation of God. I had received power from on high to live for Him and to witness for Him like His disciples had in the day of Pentecost. There is nothing that can ever compare with it. It has never left me. This power and presence of God is still with me forty years later! And it is real!

But not only did it make me **feel** good, it gave me power to witness, to preach the Gospel of Christ and to live a dedicated life serving Him as a missionary since 1947. All glory be to God.

I challenge you to seek God with a pure heart and open mind, that **you, too, might be endued with power from on high.**

MORE BOOKS FROM ENGELTAL PRESS
—GWEN SHAW'S AUTOBIOGRAPHY

UNCONDITIONAL SURRENDER—My Life Story *by Gwen R. Shaw*. Read about how this missionary evangelist received her call and the mighty anointing of the Holy Ghost which has taken her to minister in over one hundred nations of the world and carried her through a broken marriage. You will laugh and cry, but most of all, you will be challenged to your own Unconditional Surrender!
................................$17.95 Hard-cover

—THE DEEPER LIFE—

DAILY PREPARATIONS FOR PERFECTION— *by Gwen R. Shaw*. An anointed daily devotional book for the end-times. You will feel that Jesus is speaking to you every time you read it.
................................$11.95 paperback

DAY BY DAY—A Daily Praise Offering—*by Gwen R. Shaw*. Sister Gwen's latest devotional book based on the Psalms will give you an inspiring word to fill you with praise to God each day.
................................$15.95 Hard-cover

LOVE—THE LAW OF THE ANGELS—*by Gwen R. Shaw*. The message that the world needs most today is love, Love, LOVE—and the source of love is God Himself! This book gives the secret of the law that the angels live by: LOVE....................$8.95

THE MYSTERY OF THE GOLDEN RAIN—*by Gwen R. Shaw*. God has often spoken to man in parables. This is another of the earthly stories with a heavenly meaning. You will laugh and cry at this end-time message on revival and you'll never forget it!........$4.00

—IN-DEPTH BIBLE STUDIES—

SONG OF LOVE—*by Gwen R. Shaw*. This highly anointed exposition of the Song of Solomon comes from the Throne Room! Learn the love song of the Bride and the Bridegroom as the Holy Ghost teaches you verse by verse................................$7.50

GRACE ALONE—An In-Depth Bible Study on Galatians for the Serious Student of God's Word—*by Gwen R. Shaw*. Gain your freedom, in the finished work of the Cross, forsaking works which cannot add to your salvation. Be set free to live by *Grace Alone*........$11.50

MYSTERY REVEALED—An In-Depth Bible Study on Ephesians for the Serious Student of God's Word—*by Gwen R. Shaw.* Search the depth of God's riches in one of Paul's most profound epistles, "to the praise of His glory!"................................$14.75

THE LOVE LETTER—An In-Depth Bible Study on Philippians for the Serious Student of God's Word—*by Gwen R. Shaw.* You'll love this exposition on Paul's letter to the church he loved most who had ministered to him in his bonds and needed no correction...$9.00

OUR GLORIOUS HEAD—An In-Depth Bible Study on Colossians for the Serious Student of God's Word—*by Gwen R. Shaw.* An anointed study of the epistle which proclaims the glory of Christ, the Head of the Church.......................................$9.00

FORGIVE AND RECEIVE—An In-Depth Bible Study of Philemon for the Serious Student of God's Word—*by Gwen R. Shaw.* One of the smallest epistles comes alive with rich meat on the power of forgiveness..$7.00

—OTHER ANOINTED BIBLE STUDIES—

POUR OUT YOUR HEART—*by Gwen R. Shaw.* This book will transform your prayer life by leading you into a deeper place in God, making you a travailing intercessor....................$3.75

YOUR APPOINTMENT WITH GOD—*by Gwen R. Shaw.* Fasting is one of the most important keys to the power of God. Let you soul be stirred to seek God for a greater anointing in your life..$4.50

THE POWER OF THE PRECIOUS BLOOD—*by Gwen R. Shaw.* Our key to victory over Satan is the Blood of Jesus. Salvation, healing and protection are all ours because of Jesus' blood. Learn about this vital foundation stone of our faith..................$4.00

BEHOLD THE BRIDEGROOM COMETH—*by Gwen R. Shaw.* This Bible study on the soon return of Jesus deals effectively with the "Rapture" question. Our redemption draweth nigh!............$6.00

GOD'S END-TIME BATTLE PLAN—*by Gwen R. Shaw.* God has given us weapons of warfare for our spiritual battles. Learn what these weapons are and how to use them effectively............$8.00

THE FINE LINE—*by Gwen R. Shaw.* A much-needed Bible study which reveals the differences between the "soul realm" and the "spirit realm"...$6.00

ENDUED WITH LIGHT TO REIGN FOR EVER—*by Gwen R. Shaw.* God, the "Father of Lights," has created man in His image and longs for us to step out of darkness and into His light. $6.00

OUR MINISTERING ANGELS—*by Gwen R. Shaw.* A complete Bible study on the ministry of angels. Many, many questions are answered through the Word of God. This is one of the glimpses beyond the veil God is giving us in these days.................$7.50

YE SHALL RECEIVE POWER FROM ON HIGH—*by Gwen R. Shaw.* A much-needed foundational teaching on the Baptism in the Holy Spirit. Learn to teach these truths!...............$5.00

REDEEMING THE LAND *by Gwen R. Shaw.* This teaching will help you to know your authority through the blood of Jesus to break curses. A must for anyone doing spiritual warfare........$8.00

IT'S TIME FOR REVIVAL—*by Gwen R. Shaw.* Prepare your heart for the last great Revival which God is now preparing for the earth. A wonderful study on the history of revivals............$8.00

RULING IN THEIR MIDST—*by June Lewis.* Enter into the meat of the Word and learn to battle as a mature soldier of God. A unique book on spiritual warfare............................$6.00

—HEAVEN—

INTRA MUROS (Within the Gates)—*by Rebecca Ruter Springer.* This *unabridged* edition is the glorious account of an ordinary believer's visit to Heaven. A comfort to the bereaved.............$8.00

PARADISE—THE HOLY CITY AND THE GLORY OF THE THRONE—*by Elwood Scott.* You will long for the glories of your Heavenly home—as told by a man who spent 40 days there.
....$8.00

—CHILDREN'S BOOKS—

LITTLE ONES TO HIM BELONG—*by Gwen R. Shaw.* A little Chinese boy who died and went to Heaven explores the wonders of his new eternal home, escorted by Jesus................$9.75

TELL ME THE STORIES OF JESUS—*by Gwen R. Shaw.* Wonderful coloured pictures of the important events and teachings in Jesus' life, with stories as told by Gwen Shaw................$11.00

If you would like more information about this missionary organization and would like to receive our timely and informative news magazine free, write to:

END-TIME HANDMAIDENS, INC.
P. O. Box 447, Jasper, ARK 72641

PLEASE PRINT

NAME _____

STREET _____

CITY _____ STATE _____ ZIP _____

Quantity	Title	Price
	Canadians, please pay in US funds Subtotal	
	Postage and handling (see chart below)	
	Total	

ship via (check one) USPS ☐   UPS ☐

Postage and Handling Rates
U.S. Postal Service

Subtotal of order	Post./Hnd. Rates	UPS
Up to $10.00	$1.50	UPS shipping is
$10.01–$20.00	$2.00	available. Rates
$20.01–$35.00	$3.00	are calculated
$35.01–$50.00	$4.00	by weight.
$50.01 and up	$5.00	

Foreign Orders:
CANADA: Surface rate—add 50% to above postage and handling rate.
OVERSEAS: Surface rate—double the above postage and handling rate.

1/1/91   **ALL PRICES SUBJECT TO CHANGE**